THE WONDER of BIRDS

NATURE·ART·CULTURE

Edited by Dr David M. Waterhouse

Written by Dr Francesca Vanke and Dr David M. Waterhouse
with contributions by Ruth Battersby-Tooke, Dr Giorgia Bottinelli,
Dr John Davies, Dr Rosy Gray, Lisa Little, Dr Adrian Marsden,
Dr Tim Pestell and Chris Wood

Foreword by Chris Packham

Preface by Cllr George Nobbs, Leader of Norfolk County Council

Norfolk Museums Service

Contents

Front cover inspired by historic volumes in Natural History Library,
Norfolk Museums Service
Inside cover: male Common Pheasant breast feathers
Chapter heading vignettes taken from Conrad Gessner, *Historiae Animalium*,
c. 1560 in Natural History Library, Norfolk Museums Service

Edited by Dr David M. Waterhouse, Curator of Natural History
and Acting Curator of Geology, Norfolk Museums Service
Written by Dr David M. Waterhouse and Dr Francesca Vanke,
Keeper of Art and Curator of Decorative Arts, Norfolk Museums Service
Other contributing authors:
Ruth Battersby-Tooke, Curator of Costume and Textiles, Norfolk Museums Service
Dr Giorgia Bottinelli, Curator of Historic Art, Norfolk Museums Service
Dr John Davies, Chief Curator, Norfolk Museums Service
Dr Rosy Gray, Assistant Curator of Art, Norfolk Museums Service
Lisa Little, Costume and Textiles Curatorial Assistant, Norfolk Museums Service
Dr Adrian Marsden, Numismatist for the Identification and Recording Service,
at Norfolk Historic Environment Service
Dr Tim Pestell, Curator of Archaeology, Norfolk Museums Service
Chris Wood, independent researcher and volunteer, Decorative Arts Department,
Norfolk Museums Service
Foreword by Chris Packham, President, the Hawk and Owl Trust
Preface by Cllr George Nobbs, Leader, Norfolk County Council

ISBN 090310184X

Foreword

Watch a swallow bending down over a pool, slicing silently through the summer's air, flashing blue brilliance so super-fast and dipping to drink, spilling brief diamonds and then rising up and away, or stand as twilight gutters and follow the soft course of a Barn Owl as it floats in mist over a meadow, or catch the eye of a Peregrine as it stares out over Norwich and turns to peer inquisitively into the marvellous webcam which shares this species' extraordinary secrets with so many. Then in an instant you will see the wonder of birds, a wonder that has gripped our hearts for millennia and profoundly inspired and influenced so very many people.

This book acts as a companion to *The Wonder of Birds: nature, art, culture* exhibition through its presentation of a diversity of beautiful, bizarre and curious artefacts and artworks which illustrate the enduring and powerful appeal of birds. From fashion to art, from photography to archaeology, the very fact that such a wide range of references are displayed here highlights this phenomenon and both obviously and poignantly indicates just how important a role birds have played in our lives and cultures.

Yet sadly so many species are in serious decline, often flying close to the face of extinction. Swallows, Barn Owls and peregrines all face a difficult and challenging future despite the fact that we understand the intricate complex of reasons which sees them slipping away and out of our lives. And this is no good: to have the answers and to fail to effect positive change is an appalling indictment of our lethargy and will leave a terrible

legacy of loss that future generations will not thank us for. So please study these exciting 'birdy things', feel the passion, love and excitement that pulsed to see them formed and respond yourself to the simple wonder of birds. And then rise with real gusto to the challenge of their conservation so that the rich and stimulating relationships between humans and birds can prosper for years to come.

Chris Packham

President, Hawk and Owl Trust
www.hawkandowl.org

Robert Atkinson, *Sea-Watching 1952*, Left to right: Barry Spence, Graham Byford, unknown
Reproduced with permission of Moss Taylor

Preface

It is an honour to be invited to write a short preface to this exciting and attractive new book. The themes of birds and wildlife are close to the hearts of many people in Norfolk and, as the last publication from Norwich Castle, *A Vision of England* showed, there is also a long and distinguished tradition of fine art within the county.

East Anglians have a great affection for birds and have their own special names for many of them. We still call Song Thrushes 'Mavish', and the Mistle Thrush 'Fulfer', while the Bullfinch is the 'Blood-ulf', Chaffinch 'Spink' and the Yellowhammer 'Guleham' or 'Guler'. Swifts are 'Devilins' and Goldfinches have two names – 'Draw–water' and 'King Harry', and of course the Grey Heron is the 'Hanser' (which makes sense of Hamlet saying that he knows, "… a hawk from a handsaw"). So birds have a special place in our hearts, whilst our football club's name 'The Canaries' is a reflection of the affection that Norwich weavers had for this little bird that the Flemish refugees brought with them in the reign of the first Elizabeth.

East Anglia's geographic position within the UK means that it is a 'birding' hotspot. Every year thousands of tourists flock to Norfolk's 22 National Nature Reserves and 27 local Nature Reserves (not to mention the Broads National Park, and North Norfolk's Heritage Coast and Area of Outstanding Natural Beauty) in order to spot, photograph or simply to be inspired by birds.

In the pages of this book you will find wonderful works from national and regional partner institutions, such as Hans Holbein's *A Lady with a Squirrel and a Starling* from the National Gallery, London, a 17th-century watercolour of a Dodo by Pieter Holsteyn from the collections of the Natural History Museum, London, and a rare oil painting by John James Audubon entitled *Hawks Pouncing on Partridges* from the University of Liverpool Victoria Gallery & Museum. There is no doubt that these pieces are hugely impressive and important to the story of *The Wonder of Birds*, but it is the local objects and artworks covered by this book that are most appealing to me: the portrait of Sir Peter Reade, Lord Mayor of Norwich (d. 1568) with a Peregrine Falcon, from the Civic collections housed at Norwich Castle Museum & Art Gallery, the print of an Avocet and its chicks by ornithological artist Robert Gillmor from Cley-next-the-Sea in north Norfolk, and the exotic (but sadly extinct) Paradise Parakeet taxidermy specimen, collected by Frederick Strange of Aylsham and donated to the 'Norwich Museum' in 1852.

In short Norfolk Museums Service is ideally, perhaps uniquely, placed to undertake this project, and let the reader discover birds and their 'wonder' through nature, art and culture. The ambition and scope of *The Wonder of Birds* is huge, and I congratulate the contributors to this book on their dedication and determination in producing such a thorough and well-researched publication. I wholeheartedly commend this book and recommend it to anyone with an interest in birds, nature, conservation or art.

Cllr George Nobbs
Leader, Norfolk County Council

The Observatory Office 1952,
**Richard Richardson at the
Cley Bird Observatory**
Reproduced with permission of Moss Taylor

Introducing Birds

Birds are mysterious, yet familiar. This book is subtitled 'nature, art, culture' because birds are and always have been involved in all three, worldwide. Without birds, nature, art and culture would all be infinitely poorer. Of course, this subject is huge – spanning the entire time that modern humans have been on the planet. This book picks out a few of the major themes relating to birds in art and culture; acting as a companion to *The Wonder of Birds: nature, art, culture* exhibition, Norwich Castle Museum & Art Gallery (May 24th–September 18th 2014), but being equally as relevant to those readers who never saw the exhibition.

There are many books focusing on birds: from biological textbooks and bird spotters' guides, to books on the place of birds in human culture and folklore. There is no doubt that birds inspire us and leave us in awe of their beauty and character. However this book is about the results of that awe and inspiration; it is a record of some of the objects and artwork that humankind has created as a direct result of our relationship with this enigmatic group of animals (known to science as the class Aves). It celebrates the variety and beauty of birds, and illustrates some of the many roles they fulfil. It aims to convey a simple, important message: our fascination with birds transcends national and historical boundaries. More people than we can possibly imagine, from every culture, ancient and modern, at every layer of society, have loved birds. At the most basic level, birds have fed and even clothed us. Culturally they have inspired artists, writers and musicians. They have been the pets of kings and peasants, the messengers of the gods. It is the love of birds that connects a Babylonian sculptor of 2,000 BC, a 17th-century Indian emperor, and the photographer who lost an eye getting the perfect shot of a Tawny Owl in 1930s Britain!

Although exploring our relationship with birds through fine and decorative art, fashion, social history, archaeology and natural history collections – there is also a strong conservation message throughout this book. Being inspired by birds through beautiful objects and artwork so often leads to a closer understanding of the organisms themselves. Despite their cultural importance, birds are endangered. The drastic decline of so many well-known species shows we cannot take birds for granted. If we love them, we must take genuine steps to protect them. Art and culture must combine in the service of nature: to increase our understanding of birds and their habitats, and to ensure the environment is preserved for their long-term survival.

What is a bird?

Modern birds are a class of animal that includes around 10,000 living species – one of the most diverse groups of vertebrates on the planet. Birds are divided into around 30 scientific orders, consisting of over 230 families (compared with just 153 families of mammal). The Passeriformes, commonly known as songbirds or perching-birds, are the most diverse order of birds, comprising 82 families.

Birds range in weight from the Bee Hummingbird (*Mellisuga helenae*) from just 1.6 g, to the Common Ostrich (*Struthio camelus*), weighing in at up to 156.8 kg. However, the size of most birds is constrained by one limiting factor – their ability to fly.

This means that the smallest flying bird by wing area is the Bee Hummingbird (0.0007 m²) and the largest is the Andean Condor (*Vultur gryphus*) (1.06 m²).

Vultur gryphus (Andean Condor)
FAMILY **Cathartidae (New World Vultures)**
ORDER **Accipitriformes (Diurnal Birds of Prey)**

Doryfera johannae (Blue-fronted Lancebill)
FAMILY **Trochilidae (Hummingbirds)**
ORDER **Apodiformes (Swifts, Tree Swifts and Hummingbirds)**

Andean Condor and Blue-fronted Lancebill hummingbird
© Norfolk Museums Service (Norwich Castle Museum & Art Gallery)

We now know that modern birds (Neornithes) are the direct descendants of some of the dinosaurs, the rest of which died out 65 million years ago. Indeed, birds are today classed within the order Dinosauria – meaning that farmyard chickens are more closely related to the extinct *Tyrannosaurus rex* than they are to any living group, such as reptiles or mammals. It is therefore incorrect to say that dinosaurs are extinct, as they have living descendants in the form of everything from the Abd al-Kuri Sparrow (*Passer hemileucus*) to the Zone-tailed Hawk (*Buteo albonotatus*) – after all, we're still mammals, even though our very earliest mammalian ancestors have been extinct for some 225 million years. Therefore Hummingbirds and Condors (and everything in between) are all legitimate dinosaurs. Rather than referring to 'birds' and 'dinosaurs' as separate groups, dinosaur is used to describe them both, with the term 'non-avian dinosaur' describing the extinct animals that we've been used to calling dinosaurs, and 'avian dinosaur' used for what in layperson's terms might be called a bird!

The idea that birds and dinosaurs are very closely related is not a new one. As early as the 1500s anatomists noted the similarities between birds and reptiles. It wasn't until 1861 (two years after Charles Darwin published *On the Origin of Species by Means of Natural Selection*) that the first fossil evidence was unearthed to support these anatomical studies. Near Langenaltheim in Germany, a quarry worker extracting fine-grained limestone used for making lithographic plates discovered an amazing fossil, which seemed to

be halfway between a bird and a reptile. The fossil found its way to local doctor Karl Häberlein, who sold it to the British Museum, Natural History (now the Natural History Museum, London) for £700 (the equivalent of around £55,000 today). The 'London Specimen' of *Archaeopteryx lithographica* has remained at the Natural History Museum ever since. One of the reasons why this specimen is so extraordinary is that Charles Darwin himself predicted that 'transitional fossils' such as *Archaeopteryx* would eventually be found. At around 150 million years old, *Archaeopteryx* is still generally accepted as the earliest known bird, and is an important link between avian and non-avian dinosaurs.

Archaeopteryx lithographica
(meaning 'ancient wing written in stone')
FAMILY **Archaeopterygidae**
ORDER **Archaeopterygiformes**

Archaeopteryx lithographica 'London Specimen' fossil cast
© Norfolk Museums Service (Norwich Castle Museum & Art Gallery)

It used to be thought that only birds had feathers. However, one of the reasons why birds are classed as dinosaurs is because we now know that, at least some, non-avian dinosaurs had feathers. Over the last 20 years, amazing feathered non-avian dinosaur fossils have been discovered. To date, around 20 feathered non-avian dinosaur genera have been described, including *Sinosauropteryx*, *Microraptor*, *Sinornithosaurus* and *Caudipteryx*. Much work still needs to be done if we are to fully understand how birds first took to the air, but we do know that feathers evolved initially for warmth (both for adults and for brooding their young), but also for display to impress the opposite sex. From humble beginnings as little more than an insulating covering, bird feathers evolved into the infinitely complex and varied structures that we take for granted today.

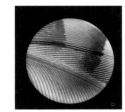

Clare Jarrett, *Feather*, 2014, limited edition digital print
© Clare Jarrett

Elephant Bird Egg

The extinct Elephant Birds (*Aepyornis* spp.) of Madagascar were the world's largest birds until their extinction, probably during the 17th century. Some Elephant Bird eggs could have a circumference of up to one metre, making them the largest ever known – even larger than the biggest sauropod dinosaurs' eggs! This plaster-of-Paris replica egg was donated by one of the founders of the Norwich Museum, John Henry Gurney Sr. (1819–1890) in 1857. In the same donation J. H. Gurney also gave an identical replica egg plus a cast of an Elephant Bird's leg bones, standing 1.6 metres at the hip!

The English name 'Elephant Bird' may have originated simply because of the bird's large size (an animal of elephantine proportions), or possibly from Marco Polo's 1298 account of the Roc (or Rukh), which was believed to be a bird large enough to seize an elephant in its talons. Either way, the legendary Roc and real Elephant Bird have been confounded throughout history. Until its extinction during the 15th century Madagascar was also home to the Malagasy Crowned Eagle, *Stephanoaetus mahery* (closely related to the extant African Crowned Eagle *Stephanoaetus coronatus*).

Another hypothesis relates to the fact that adult Elephant Birds (along with other birds within the Ratite group) have certain paedomorphic features – that is to say that apart from their size, the adults resemble the young of other birds. After seeing fully grown Elephant Birds, sailors may have speculated that they were the chicks of an enormous eagle-like bird!

Aepyornis sp. (Elephant Bird)
FAMILY Aepyornithidae (Elephant Birds)
ORDER Aepyornithiformes (Elephant Birds)

Stephanoaetus coronatus (African Crowned Eagle)
FAMILY Accipitridae (Hawks, Eagles, Kites, Harriers and Old World Vultures)
ORDER Accipitriformes (Diurnal Birds of Prey)

An Elephant Bird next to a Common Ostrich for scale
© David M. Waterhouse

Alfred Waterhouse, *Dodo design for museums interior*, 1870s, pencil on paper
© The Trustees of the Natural History Museum, London

Dodo Design

Dodos are synonymous with extinction, being used as a byword for something dead, destroyed or long-gone. It was Dutch sailors who discovered the island of Mauritius in 1598 and brought back stories of the species. The last confirmed sighting of a living Dodo was just 64 years later in 1662, although the species could conceivably have survived into the 1690s.

Alfred Waterhouse (1830–1905), the young architect of the Natural History Museum's main building in South Kensington, based this design for a terracotta ornament on a painting by Roelant Savery (c. 1626) held in the museum's collections. Although this way of portraying Dodos is familiar to us, we now know it is inaccurate. Because most early illustrations of Dodos were copied from 'overstuffed' taxidermy specimens produced by taxidermists who had never seen the living birds, the image of fat, squat, lumbering birds has persisted to this day.

Raphus cucullatus (Dodo)
FAMILY **Columbidae (Pigeons and Doves)**
ORDER **Columbiformes (Pigeons and Doves)**

Dodo Extinction Factors

Dr Julian Hume is a palaeontologist, artist and writer who specializes in reconstructing extinct bird species. His main research area focuses on the Mascarene Islands of Mauritius, Réunion and Rodrigues, where research for his PhD on the palaeontology of Dodos and other extinct animals took him. Through scientific study of the remains of this enigmatic extinct bird, Hume's reconstructions of Dodos are more accurate than anything previously produced.

When Mauritius was discovered, it was a paradise of freshwater lagoons filled with fish, and forests rich in palms and other trees. Because no humans set foot on the island before 1598 the lush vegetation contained birds without any fear of humans. Together with the copious amounts of valuable Ebony trees (*Diospyros* spp.), the island soon became a much-visited stop-off point for merchant ships. Within 100 years of its discovery, Mauritius was altered beyond recognition, and many endemic species such as the Dodo became extinct. Although its lack of fear of humans and flightlessness would have made it easy pickings as a food source for sailors, it was the introduction of alien species to the island that ultimately led to the extinction of the Dodo. This painting depicts Mauritius as it would have looked during the 1650s or 1660s; rife with introduced animals such as Pigs (*Sus scrofa domesticus*), Crab-eating Macaques (*Macaca fascicularis*), Cats (*Felis* [*silvestris*] *catus*), Black Rats (*Rattus rattus*) and Javan Rusa Deer (*Rusa timorensis*). It also illustrates deforestation by humans for Ebony wood, and burning native vegetation in order to make way for agriculture.

Julian Pender Hume,
Dodo Extinction Factors,
2014, acrylic on paper
(and detail opposite)
© Julian Pender Hume

Julian Pender Hume,
*A day in the life;
Mare aux Songes,
4000 YBP*, 2006,
acrylic
© Julian Pender Hume

Pieter Holsteyn, *Portrait of White Dodo,* c.1670s,
watercolour on paper

Victorian 'overstuffed' Dodo (left)
and modern scientific view (right)

Portrait of White Dodo

This intriguing watercolour by Pieter Holsteyn
(1614–1687) was painted around 1670. It was
once thought to have been produced by his father,
Pieter Pietersz Holsteyn (1585–1662), from bird(s)
that were brought back alive to the artists' native
Holland. This Victorian misconception led to a
whole host of further errors, culminating in the
widely held, but totally erroneous, belief that a
white Dodo once existed on the island of Réunion
(about 200 kilometres southwest of Mauritius).
Despite sketchy evidence, the fictitious 'Réunion
White Dodo' was even given a scientific name
– *Raphus solitarius*.

Thanks to research by Dr Julian Hume and
Dr Anthony Cheke, we now know that, just like
the Waterhouse representations of Dodos, this
illustration was based on a painting by Roelant
Savery. Savery's original, produced in Prague in
1611, was painted from a taxidermy specimen
that once formed part of Holy Roman Emperor
Rudolf II's (1552–1612) curiosity collection.
This specimen was whitish in colour, and
probably represented a rare albinistic Mauritian
Dodo. Indeed, Hume and Cheke conclude that
"… it is likely that dodos in Mauritius had already
lost the power of flight before neighbouring
Réunion emerged from the seabed", making
the possibility of a Réunion Dodo (white or
otherwise) completely unfeasible.

Laughing Owl

When this bird specimen was collected from the South Island of New Zealand in the 1890s, this species of endemic owl was already critically endangered. By 1914 the last recorded specimen was found dead in Canterbury on New Zealand's South Island. Although officially described as 'extinct', there have been a number of unconfirmed sightings of Laughing Owls during the 1920s, 1940s and 1960s (including apparently fresh Laughing Owl egg fragments found in the Canterbury region in 1960). Most intriguingly of all, in 1985 a group of Americans camping in the remote Timaru District of New Zealand's South Island reported hearing the sound of a 'madman laughing' during the night. At the time unexplained, due to the fact that there seemed to be no other person for miles around, this noise has since been interpreted as possibly a Laughing Owl call. Despite sounding far-fetched, stranger things have happened – the phenomenon of 'Lazarus taxa' is well documented, and refers to organisms that although apparently extinct for years, are actually rediscovered alive. The most famous example of a 'Lazarus taxon' is the Coelacanth fish (*Latimeria* spp.), which despite previously being known only from fossil remains (and thought to have died out 66 million years ago), was discovered in 1938 living off the coast of South Africa. However, less extreme cases have also been recognized, such as the South Island Takahē (*Porphyrio hochstetteri*) a large flightless bird in the rail family, which was thought to have become extinct in 1898, but was rediscovered alive in 1948.

© Norfolk Museums Service (Norwich Castle Museum & Art Gallery)

Sceloglaux albifacies (Laughing Owl)
FAMILY **Strigidae (Typical Owls)**
ORDER **Strigiformes (Owls)**

South Island Takahē
© David M. Waterhouse

Passenger Pigeon

2014 marks the centenary of extinction for another bird – although unfortunately the Passenger Pigeon is far less likely than the Laughing Owl to be rediscovered alive in the wild. The story of the Passenger Pigeon is made all the more incredible by the fact that at one stage, it was probably the most numerous bird on the planet. A single flock of these birds described in Ontario, Canada, in 1866, was said to have been nearly a kilometre wide and 480 kilometres long (taking 14 hours to pass overhead) – consisting of an estimated 3.5 billion birds!

Ultimately the species' downfall was its breeding habits. After migrating many thousands of kilometres ranging from most of the mid, south, north and eastern United States and south-eastern Canada, they would settle in their breeding grounds in the deciduous forests of the eastern United States in March to May. Each of these colonies was known as a 'city', and would typically be in forested areas covering 1300 square kilometres or more. Numbers fell steadily during the early 19th century due to deforestation of breeding areas. By the 1870s a disastrous decline had started in Passenger Pigeon numbers due to hunting on an unprecedented scale. Pigeon meat was seen as a cheap food for slaves and the poor, and the expansion of the railroads in the mid-19th century made it easier to ship huge quantities of pigeons to cities such as Boston, New York and Philadelphia. The adult birds were shot out of the sky thousands at a time, and the young (known as squabs) were shaken straight out of their nesting trees, or even had the trees cut down from under them.

Julian Pender Hume, *Passenger Pigeon hunt, 1875*, 2012, acrylic
© Julian Pender Hume

Despite conservation laws being passed in several states during the late-19th century, they were rarely enforced. Numbers had become so low in the 1890s that even if the laws had been complied with, the species could not have been saved from extinction. The bird's breeding strategy based on 'safety in numbers' meant that small groups of Passenger Pigeons could not initiate courtship, and therefore did not breed. Sadly, the last known Passenger Pigeon (known as 'Martha'), died in Cincinnati Zoo on September 1st 1914.

Ectopistes migratorius (Passenger Pigeon)
FAMILY **Columbidae (Pigeons and Doves)**
ORDER **Columbiformes**
(Pigeons and Doves)

Map showing former wintering zone (yellow) and breeding zone (blue) of Passenger Pigeons

© Norfolk Museums Service
(Lynn Museum)

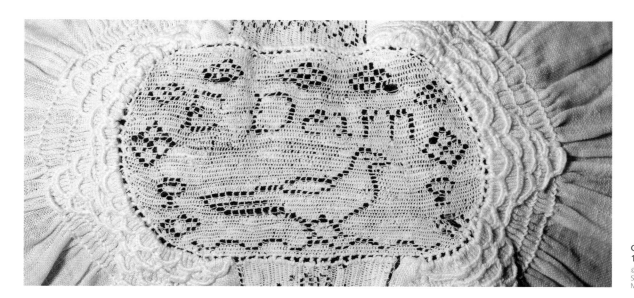

Dove Christening Cap

There is a strong tradition of representing the Holy Spirit as a dove. Indeed in the Bible, the Holy Spirit is said to have descended upon Jesus like a dove during his baptism in the River Jordan (Matthew 3:16). The motif of the Holy Dove was especially prevalent during the Renaissance period: from Pietro Perugino's *Baptism of Christ* (c. 1482) and Peter Paul Rubens' *The Annunciation* (1608–1628) to Bartolomé Esteban Murillo's *Die beiden Dreieinigkeiten* (1675–1682) to name but a few examples. Because of this connection between the Holy Dove and baptism, doves later became popular motifs associated with christenings. When christening caps and gowns became prevalent in the 18th and early 19th century, a dove was the obvious choice of needlework embellishment to decorate these items.

Hollie Point (or Holy Point) is often regarded as the only true form of English lace, as it was an exclusively English technique from the 16th to the 19th century. Ostensibly a detailed and complex stitch technique made using buttonhole stitches running in rows to form intricate designs, it is thought that the method (sometimes also known as 'Nuns' Work') was originally used in nunneries and monasteries. It lends itself to embellishment on small items of clothing and is found most commonly on baby clothes and baptismal attire. Perhaps unsurprisingly, Hollie Point motifs often have biblical or religious connotations: in this case it is worked in the form of the Holy Dove, alongside the name 'E. Dearn'. Later examples found on cuffs, collars, samplers and underwear/nightwear insertions, reveal that the technique became a very personal and domestic art.

Columba livia domestica (Domestic Dove)
FAMILY **Columbidae (Pigeons and Doves)**
ORDER **Columbiformes (Pigeons and Doves)**

Darwin's Egg

The only egg known to have survived from Charles Darwin's famous HMS *Beagle* voyage during the 1830s. This egg, most probably from a Spotted Nothura Tinamou (*Nothura maculosa*), was collected in Uruguay only to be rediscovered by a volunteer at the University Museum of Zoology, Cambridge, in 2009, which was coincidentally the 200th anniversary of Darwin's birth. The egg clearly has the name 'C. Darwin' written on it, and records show that the large crack on the egg's surface was caused when Darwin packed it in a box which was too small for it!

Nothura maculosa
(Spotted Nothura Tinamou)
FAMILY **Tinamidae**
(Tinamous)
ORDER **Tinamiformes**
(Tinamous)

Tinamou egg collected during Charles Darwin's HMS *Beagle* voyage, 1830s

A Lady with a Squirrel and a Starling

This unique painting by Hans Holbein the Younger encapsulates many of the ideas explored in this book, concerning birds and their symbolism. The Starling is essential to the picture's meaning, a vital visual pointer to identifying the family and location of the sitter, recently and convincingly argued to be Lady Anne Lovell from East Harling in Norfolk. The Starling is subtly portrayed in dark colours, in contrast with the striking pale shawl and hood of the woman. However, the iridescence of the feathers is portrayed with the same delicacy and observational genius that typifies Holbein's approach to his human subjects, and the Starling's bright eye and alert expression as it looks towards its owner renders it full of character. The bird is an active personality within the composition.

The painting illustrates ways in which birds could be incorporated into Tudor portraiture: partly fulfilling an almost heraldic role, partly as a visual pun. The work's Norfolk provenance and ostensible Norfolk sitter add an intriguing layer of interest to the painting when seen from an East Anglian point of view.

Sturnus vulgaris
(Common Starling)
FAMILY
Sturnidae (Starlings)
ORDER **Passeriformes**
(Perching Birds)

Hans Holbein the Younger (c. 1497–1543), *A Lady with a Squirrel and a Starling (Anne Lovell?)*, c. 1526–1528, oil on oak, 560 x 388 mm

Goldfinch Taxidermy and X-ray

Fred Ashton (1908–1976) was apprenticed to Frederick Ernest Gunn (1869–1950). F. E. Gunn was in turn an apprentice of his father Thomas Edward Gunn (1844–1923) and the Gunn taxidermy style formed the basis of the 'Norwich School of Taxidermy', which ultimately derived from John Sayer (1815–1866) 'Animal and Bird Preserver, St. Giles, Norwich'. Gunns' apprenticeships lasted for five years and came with some harsh conditions, such as to, "… obey his master's lawful command, keep his master's secrets, not play cards or dice, not frequent music halls or taverns, and not get married"!

However, it was as an independent taxidermist that Fred became most notorious – he famously ate the meat of the animals that he worked on. Indeed, the old floorboards Fred often used as bases for taxidermy still have written in pencil on them, simply, 'I ate body'!

More often used for medical reasons, radiography using X-rays is a useful tool in the study of historical taxidermy. Taxidermy labels can become lost or destroyed, and taxidermy can be taken out of original cases. There are a number of clues that can be used in order to gain an idea of who originally produced the taxidermy. One clue is the internal wire-work which is inserted to keep the piece in position – most of the skeleton and soft tissue is removed, and wires and a body made from wood shavings, cotton wool and other natural fibres is made as a replacement. X-rays can be used in order to assess the internal structure, so that the unique way of wiring the specimen can be seen without destroying it. In this case the 'Norwich School' system of a single wire through the legs and bent around in the head can clearly be seen.

Carduelis carduelis (European Goldfinch)
FAMILY **Fringillidae (True Finches)**
ORDER **Passeriformes (Perching Birds)**

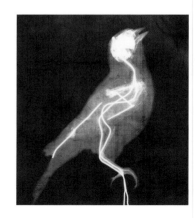

Landscape of Shame

In this work the pathetic group of dead birds strewn about the field forms a startling, heart-rending incursion into what should be an unremarkable, traditional agricultural landscape. A scene that appears at first sight to be surreal fantasy is, in fact, reality. Cedric Morris (1889–1982) clearly intended the shame of the title to be felt by the viewer as this work portrays starkly the situation in which he found himself at the time, subjected to the continual sight of birds in the Suffolk countryside suffering from the deadly effects of pollution. DDT, used frequently as an agricultural insecticide during the 1950s and 1960s, resulted in birds literally dropping dead in the fields. Here they appear like corpses on a battlefield, losers in the war of man versus nature.

This work by an important East Anglian artist who was also a passionate bird lover, forms a hard-hitting link between conservation and art. Its direct appeal to the emotions is elicited not by dramatic hyperbole, but by unadorned realism.

DDT

Birds were key in the discovery that DDT and other insecticides were damaging to the environment. During the 1950s researchers in the USA first noticed that where DDT was being used to control beetles spreading Dutch Elm Disease, birds such as American Robins (*Turdus migratorius*) were dying in their millions.

One of the ways in which DDT affects birds is that even if relatively small amounts are being ingested, over time the pesticides build up in the birds' systems. This is even more pronounced in apex predators such as birds of prey, as they eat other birds already containing concentrations of DDT-related chemicals. The chemicals then alter the birds' calcium metabolism, ultimately resulting in thin eggshells and an inability to produce offspring.

For example, by the early 1970s Peregrine Falcons (*Falco peregrinus*) were extinct in the eastern United States and south-eastern Canada. Museum egg collections were used in order to prove the link between DDT and eggshell thinning in birds. This study led to a total DDT ban in the United States in 1972, and in 1984 in the UK. Thankfully, populations of this species and others on both sides of the Atlantic are now slowly recovering.

Frederick Sandys, *Drawing of a brambling finch*, 1842–1844, watercolour on paper
© Norfolk Museums Service (Norwich Castle Museum & Art Gallery)

Brambling Taxidermy and Watercolour

Bramblings are a migratory finch common in the UK from September to March. Although very similar in habit, size and shape to Chaffinches (*Fringilla coelebs*), Bramblings seek out beech mast (Beech tree nuts) during the winter, to avoid competition with their close relatives. This taxidermy specimen is leucistic – meaning that its plumage lacks most of the melanin pigment that produces browns and black, whilst carotenoid pigments, responsible for yellows and oranges, are unaffected. Abnormal pigmentation such as leucism and albinism can result in weak feathers, which are more prone to wear.

This can hinder flight, as well as making the birds more conspicuous to predators. It can even affect recognition by potential mates.

The Victorians were fascinated by unusual forms of wild birds, and these examples fetched higher prices than the 'normal' specimens. Museum taxidermy collections dating from the 19th century can sometimes contain more unusual colour variants than the more usual forms we are used to seeing in the wild.

Norwich-born Frederick Sandys (1829–1904) is best known today for his portraits in the pre-Raphaelite tradition. Local banker and founder of the Norwich Museum, J. H. Gurney Sr. commissioned Sandys to paint watercolours of interesting and important taxidermy specimens from the Museum. Some of these paintings are labelled with the word 'Museum', but most of the original taxidermy no longer survives in the collection. This distinctive colour-variant Brambling is the last taxidermy piece known to be in existence out of the large folio of originals that Sandys painted.

Fringilla montifringilla (Brambling)
FAMILY **Fringillidae**
(True Finches)
ORDER **Passeriformes**
(Perching Birds)

© Norfolk Museums Service
(Norwich Castle Museum & Art Gallery)

Pietre Dure Cabinet

This cabinet was made to house a collection of small and precious objects, such as antique cameos, gems and/or fossils. It is decorated with panels of cut and shaped marble and other precious and semi-precious stones. This type of stone mosaic is an Italian speciality known as *pietre dure* or 'hard stones'. Rare and beautiful natural materials combined with dazzling craftsmanship represented a harmonious union of nature and man, closely reflecting many early collectors' artistic and intellectual interests.

   The panels on this cabinet feature naturalistic representations of birds, fruit and flowers. Most collectors of the 17th and 18th centuries were equally interested in both natural history and the arts, and so the decorations on the outside of the cabinet probably reflected the nature of its contents. Here both the bright colours and subtle speckled shades of the stones have been used with equally dazzling effect to create realistic renderings of different species of bird, both recognizable such as Goldfinches (*Carduelis carduelis*) but also more fantastical birds, to create an exuberant whole.

ORDER **Passeriformes**
(Perching Birds)

© Norfolk Museums Service
(Norwich Castle Museum
& Art Gallery)

Andrea Mantegna, *Bird on a Branch*, c. 1470s–1480s

Bird on a Branch

Andrea Mantegna's (c. 1431–1506) *Bird on a Branch* beautifully combines acute observation with the sculptural quality typical of Mantegna's work in all media. Very few of Mantegna's designs for decorative objects survive, but this bird, perhaps part of a pair with the similar example in the National Gallery of Art in Washington, could have been intended for an engraving or decorative carving.

Mantegna's drawing shows how, although he is best known today for his monumental, classically influenced paintings, this artist's work could be exuberantly decorative, as well as sensitive in his expression of the bird's lively character. This is the earliest drawing featured within this book, and contrasts with later artists' approaches. Interestingly, the bird depicted does not seem to be of any recognizable species, and it may be that Mantegna has used his imagination to portray a bird that combines features of several different types into one.

ORDER **Passeriformes (Perching Birds)**

Rose Croix **Masonic Apron**

Pelicans have a long symbolic history in both Christian culture and Medieval heraldry. This was brought about by the mistaken belief that mother pelicans were so devoted to their young that they would peck their breast when food was not available, feeding their chicks on their own blood. This belief may have begun because pelicans sometimes press their bills to their chests in order to fully empty their gular pouches of food and/or water. In addition, the Dalmatian Pelican (*Pelecanus crispus*) of central and southeastern Asia, the Middle East and eastern Europe, develops a vivid orange-red pouch during the breeding season, which may have contributed to the myth. Whichever way the legend came about, it is widely held that the pelican is symbolically feeding her young with her blood, just as Jesus Christ shed his blood to save mankind.

However, the original significance of the pelican, as well as its meaning within Freemasonry, may be slightly different, in that the mother pelican's blood is said to resurrect her young rather than saving them – the chicks having been killed by their father (representing evil).

This type of apron (a part of the regalia or ceremonial clothing worn in Freemasonry) is no longer used in England and Wales. It would have been worn by an 18th degree mason, of the Christian *Rose Croix* order (or 'The Ancient and Accepted Rite for England and Wales and its Districts and Chapters Overseas', to give it its official title!).

© Norfolk Museums Service (Norwich Castle Museum & Art Gallery)

FAMILY **Pelecanidae (Pelicans)**
ORDER **Pelecaniformes (Pelicans, Herons, Shoebill Stork and Spoonbills)**

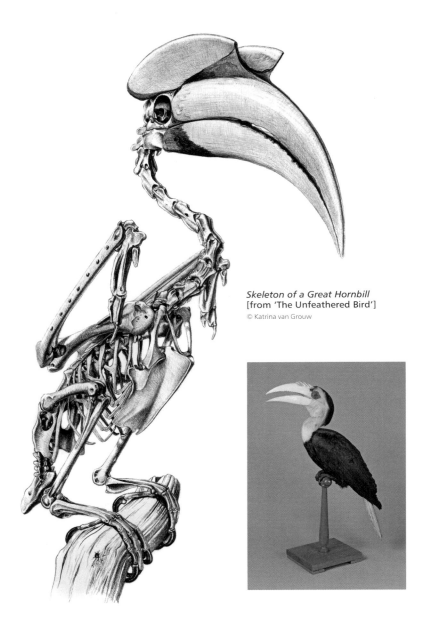

Skeleton of a Great Hornbill
[from 'The Unfeathered Bird']
© Katrina van Grouw

Skeleton of a Great Hornbill

Katrina van Grouw's (b. 1965) work bridges art, science and history; having worked as a Curator of Birds at the Natural History Museum's Bird Group in Tring, Hertfordshire, she is also a skilled natural history illustrator. Her fascinatingly detailed illustrations may have a dream-like quality, but are precise anatomical drawings, and go a long way to explaining the 'wonder' of birds in the natural world. Her works reveal what goes on 'under the skin', showing a bird's underlying structure, and how the skeleton of a species may be uniquely adapted for its habitat and lifestyle. This Great Hornbill – one of the most impressive and well-known species of India and South East Asia – is a spectacular example of van Grouw's work. The skeleton of this species shows the large, distinctive casque above its bill, while the hollow bones assist this heavy bird to fly, keeping its weight sufficiently low to allow it to be airborne: an evolutionary advantage birds have over human beings!

Buceros bicornis (Great Hornbill)
and *Rhyticeros subruficollis*
(Plain-pouched Hornbill)
FAMILY **Bucerotidae (Hornbills)**
ORDER **Coraciiformes (Kingfishers, Hoopoe, Bee-eaters, Rollers and Hornbills)**

Plain-pouched Hornbill
© Norfolk Museums Service
(Norwich Castle Museum & Art Gallery)

Predators and Prey

(including Falconiformes, Strigiformes and Galliformes)

Birds encompass many different qualities. Some species are awe-inspiring natural predators, which have long been valued by mankind. This chapter explores falconry as a high-status pastime amongst royalty and nobility past and present, with the possession of birds of prey being a mark of rank in cultures across the world. Apart from their abilities as hunters, the sheer strength and ferocity of birds like eagles has led to them being endowed with great symbolic power. They are associated with divinity, kingship and nationhood. The owl, conversely, although just as fierce a hunter, has a far more ambiguous reputation, because of its nocturnal habit and eerie hoot and screech.

Every bird can easily become prey, and the human race is their chief predator. We kill birds in their thousands, for food or, far less justifiably, for prestigious 'trophies'. We pollute land and destroy nests and habitats for our convenience, endangering many once-abundant species. Conservation organizations work to increase numbers of endangered species, and reintroduce them where they have dwindled. When that species is a predatory one, such as the White-tailed Eagle (*Haliaeetus albicilla*), problems can follow as the existing balance is changed.

It is ironic that top predators such as hawks, eagles and owls symbolize strength and power, but in practice often hold extremely fragile roles within ecosystems. These 'apex predators' are fewer in number than their prey, and can easily be affected by pollutants, habitat destruction and persecution by humans.

It is difficult to maintain the delicate balance between our needs and those of birds, whether predators or prey. There is no easy answer, but that does not excuse us from making the attempt! One example of a success story is the ongoing work with Peregrine Falcons (*Falco peregrinus*) by the *Hawk and Owl Trust*: in the 1950s there were just 400 pairs of peregrines in the UK due to persecution as well as the effects of toxic agricultural chemicals such as DDT. Due to concerted conservation efforts, there are now 1,400 breeding pairs in the country. After an absence of over 100 years, Peregrine Falcons are once more breeding in Norwich, thanks to a nest platform installed by the *Hawk and Owl Trust* on Norwich Cathedral spire.

The Cawston Chalice Case

This remarkable survival from the pre-Reformation period is made from boiled leather, known as *cuir-bouilli*. It may have been intended to hold either a chalice for the celebration of the Mass, or possibly a ceremonial crown for a statue of St Agnes.

The lid is decorated with a beautifully tooled image of a griffin. This is a legendary beast with the body, back legs and tail of a Lion (*Panthera leo*) and the head, wings and talons of an eagle (family Accipitridae). It was depicted frequently in ancient Greece and Achaemenid Persia, as well as in Medieval European and Islamic art. The combination of two such strong, majestic creatures imbued it with immense symbolic power. It was used heraldically to denote kingship, or talismanically as protection from evil. In the Medieval world it was believed to have the power to guard gold and other treasure. On this leather case, the Griffin's symbolism is the visual key to its use: strongly suggesting the creature was placed there to protect the precious object inside.

There are other part-eagle fantastic beasts in both eastern and western mythologies, including the Hippogriff, Anzû and Simurgh. These testify to the power of the eagle in the human mind, and the reverence ascribed to it as king of birds.

Simurgh: part dog or lion and part eagle or peacock
© David M. Waterhouse

Part eagle, part lion demi-god Anzû
© David M. Waterhouse

On loan from Church of St Agnes, Cawston, Norfolk © Norfolk Museums Service (Norwich Castle Museum & Art Gallery)

Eric Hosking, *Barn Owl*, 1933
© The Eric Hosking Charitable Trust

Eric Hosking's Barn Owls

Eric Hosking (1909–1991) was an internationally important pioneering bird photographer. He did much of his work in East Anglia, and is particularly known for his love of owls. His lifelong passion for these birds is perhaps remarkable since he lost an eye in 1937 when a Tawny Owl (*Strix aluco*) attacked him during a photo shoot!

During the 1930s Hosking addressed the then difficult issue of how to photograph nocturnal species. This series of three owl images shows how the development of flash photography revolutionized the way in which nocturnal birds could be portrayed. This first picture, from 1933, shows a Barn Owl hunting in daylight. Although usually dawn and dusk hunters, these Owls sometimes hunt during the day, especially in winter. In the early 1930s it would have been the only time possible to capture an image of the bird.

During the 1930s and 1940s Hosking experimented with flash photography, and pioneered methods that allowed him to use high-speed flashes to freeze movement. This second photograph was taken in Suffolk in 1936. Hosking illuminated what would have been a pitch-dark space by setting off a flash by hand – by pure chance, at exactly the right moment, capturing the owl with its prey! The speed of the flash, as Hosking himself noted, was not sufficient to arrest the movement in the rat's tail, which appears blurred as a consequence.

The dramatic image of a Barn Owl taken in 1948 is the result of an early use of auto-trip triggering the flash. This is activated by the bird's own movement, allowing the camera to capture this dynamic pose. This was Hosking's own favourite owl image, and probably one of his most well known worldwide. The speed of this later flash is much higher than the one used in the previous image. It has captured every detail of the image crisply and clearly, down to the tail of the vole the owl holds in its beak!

Tyto alba (Barn Owl)
FAMILY **Tytonidae (Barn Owls)**
ORDER **Strigiformes (Owls)**

Eric Hosking,
Barn Owl, 1936
© The Eric Hosking Charitable Trust

Eric Hosking,
Heraldic Barn Owl, 1948
© The Eric Hosking Charitable Trust

Owl Jug

Owls have complex, often ambivalent symbolism. In the Classical Greek world they carried positive connotations as the symbol of the goddess Athena. In some parts of ancient China, the owl was a deity that featured in creation myths. However, its most common Early Modern European meaning was as a messenger of ill omen and death. As a nocturnal bird it was also a vehicle of anti-Semitism, symbolizing the Jews who (as it was thought at the time) chose to live in the 'darkness' of non-belief, as opposed to the 'light' of Christianity.

However, despite this not always positive symbolism, the unique physical qualities of owls have also been an inspiration in the fine and applied arts in a less serious context. In this work the ceramicist has wittily interpreted the owl's plump, compact shape as a jug, with its round head as a cup. The slip decoration, although almost naïve in its simplicity, nonetheless recognizably renders the speckled feather pattern of the Tawny Owl, while the creature's saucer-like eyes perfectly convey the endearingly surprised expression typical of the species.

The wide range of artistic renditions, ancient and modern, of this extraordinary group of birds, demonstrates the enduring fascination of the owl to artist and maker, and the endless possibilities for the interpretation of its form and character – from solemn to sinister to humorous.

© Norfolk Museums Service (Norwich Castle Museum & Art Gallery)

Strix aluco (Tawny Owl)
FAMILY **Strigidae** (Typical Owls)
ORDER **Strigiformes** (Owls)

Owl jug, *c.* 1680–1700
© The Fitzwilliam Museum, Cambridge

Hawk Pouncing on Partridges

The lasting importance of John James Audubon (1785–1851), both to ornithological study and to the depiction of birds in art, cannot be over-estimated. He pioneered naturalistic methods of interpretation of the birds he studied, drawing only fresh specimens, rather than from taxidermy as was the norm at the time. He was the first artist to attempt to portray birds in natural contexts rather than stiffly posed. At the same time, he vividly communicated the emotional impact of the compositions he recreated. No book on birds would be complete without reference to Audubon's seminal *Birds of America*. The painting, a direct copy of Plate 76 from this work, encompasses all the major characteristics of Audubon's approach: the meticulous attention to detail, combined with a Romantic emphasis on the tragic drama of the event, reflecting his firm belief that the naturalist must also be an artist.

Buteo lineatus (Red-shouldered Hawk)
FAMILY **Accipitridae (Hawks, Eagles, Kites, Harriers and Old World Vultures)**
ORDER **Accipitriformes (Diurnal Birds of Prey)**

Colinus virginianus (Northern Bobwhite)
FAMILY **Odontophoridae (New World Quails)**
ORDER **Galliformes (Gamebirds)**

John James Audubon, *Hawk Pouncing on Partridges, c.* 1827
Reproduced with the kind permission of University of Liverpool Victoria Gallery & Museum

John James Audubon
aged around 75

Hawk and Owl Trust

Hawk and Owl Trust

Founded in 1969 amid increasing concern due to the alarming decline in peregrines and other raptor numbers, the *Hawk and Owl Trust* is a UK-based conservation charity dedicated to conserving birds of prey in the wild. The trust's other aims are to increase knowledge and appreciation of birds of prey amongst the general public, as well as to manage wildlife reserves and education centres, and to create and manage nesting, roosting and feeding habitats.

One such nest site that has had considerable success in recent years was installed on Norwich Cathedral's iconic spire in 2011. Famously featured as part of insurance company Aviva's (formerly Norwich Union) logo, Norwich Cathedral spire is perhaps now better known for its Peregrine Falcons! The falcons first appeared at the Cathedral in 2009 when a male peregrine took up residence on the spire. A female soon followed and the *Hawk and Owl Trust*, working in partnership with Norwich Cathedral, set up a nesting platform, along with two webcams. The breeding pair successfully fledged chicks in 2012 and 2013 and indications are that they are set to have similar success during 2014.

Along with the obvious success of fledging chicks boosting the UK number of wild peregrines, it was the installation of the webcams that has proved hugely influential for the Trust's aim to increase knowledge and appreciation of the birds. Adding to Norwich Cathedral's Refectory viewing point, Norwich Castle Museum & Art Gallery also boasts a live feed from the nest platform for the duration of *The Wonder of Birds* exhibition, summer 2014.

© Hawk and Owl Trust, Andy Thompson

The live online webcam has attracted attention from around the world, with over 3.5 million views to date.

Peregrine Falcons' natural habitats are high rocky areas, such as mountains and cliffs. Ironically the 'Norwich Cathedral Peregrines' have found a new home in England's least mountainous county – Norfolk! This is less surprising than it first sounds, as increasingly peregrines are moving into cities, where persecution and pesticides are lower, and huge populations of Feral Pigeons (*Columba livia*) live. Tall buildings are perfect substitutes for rocky cliffs, and 80% or more of city peregrines' diet consists of pigeons.

Falco peregrinus (Peregrine Falcon)
FAMILY Falconidae (Falcons and Caracaras)
ORDER Falconiformes (Falcons and Caracaras)

© Hawk and Owl Trust, Andy Thompson

Red-legged Partridge

At first glance this piece of taxidermy seems unremarkable. Its true relevance is only revealed through the accompanying information. This Red-legged (or French) Partridge is the oldest piece of taxidermy in Norfolk Museums Service's collections. Incredibly, considering its condition, it dates from December 1790!

This species was only introduced into the country earlier that same year. In 1790 both the Earl of Bristol and Baron Rendlesham imported Red-legged Partridge eggs to their Suffolk estates from the Continent, and the young birds quickly escaped and spread into Norfolk. The Red-legged Partridge has since become a common feature of this region's landscape, but this specimen must be one of the first ever to live, and be shot, in East Anglia.

Alectoris rufa (Red-legged Partridge)
FAMILY **Phasianidae (Pheasants, Partridges, Junglefowl and Peafowl)**
ORDER **Galliformes (Gamebirds)**

Anonymous,
Sir Peter Reade,
undated,
oil on panel,
© Norfolk Museums
Service (Norwich Castle
Museum & Art Gallery)

Sir Peter Reade

Sir Peter Reade was a wealthy mercer and a Lord Mayor of prosperous Tudor Norwich. Although of the merchant class rather than a nobleman by birth, Reade had been knighted by the Holy Roman Emperor, Charles V, for military service, and here his falcon may be seen as a mark of rank. The hood on the bird's head makes it difficult to identify positively, but it most closely resembles a Peregrine Falcon, a perennially important and prestigious bird for the sport of hawking. By the Tudor period, the earlier Medieval hierarchies which considered a peregrine to be a suitable bird for an earl rather than a mere knight would have been less current. However, to his contemporaries, Reade's possession of a peregrine would still have indicated a high position in society.

Falco peregrinus (Peregrine Falcon)
FAMILY **Falconidae (Falcons and Caracaras)**
ORDER **Falconiformes (Falcons and Caracaras)**

RANK	ASSIGNED BIRD
King	Eagles (*Aquila* spp.), Gyrfalcon (*Falco rusticolus*)
Prince	Juvenile Gyrfalcon (*Falco rusticolus*)
Duke	Female Peregrine Falcon (*Falco peregrinus*)
Earl	Male Peregrine Falcon (*Falco peregrinus*)
Baron	Common Buzzard (*Buteo buteo*)
Knight	Saker Falcon (*Falco cherrug*)
Esquire	Lanner Falcon (*Falco biarmicus*)
Lady	Merlin (*Falco columbarius*)
Youngman	Eurasian Hobby (*Falco subbuteo*)
Yeoman (cook)	Female Northern Goshawk (*Accipiter gentilis*)
Poorman	Male Northern Goshawk (*Accipiter gentilis*)
Priest	Female Eurasian Sparrowhawk (*Accipiter nisus*)
Clerk	Male Eurasian Sparrowhawk (*Accipiter nisus*)
Knave	Common Kestrel (*Falco tinnunculus*)

The *Boke of Seynt Albans* (Book of Saint Albans) of 1486 explained common gentlemanly pursuits of the day; namely hawking, hunting and heraldry. This table is a summary of one reproduced within the book. Although Sir Peter Reade's portrait was painted some 80 years after the *Boke of Seynt Albans* was published, it does highlight the status he had attained. Even if he wasn't an Earl or a Duke, Sir Peter Reade was certainly of a high enough social standing to warrant an equally impressive bird.

Hawking Vervels

Vervels are the metal loops that were used to connect the leather 'jesses' or straps on a hawk's legs to their stands or leashes. The word derives from the Old French *vervelle*, attested in 1350, indicating the early origin to these items in falconry. They were usually inscribed with the name of the bird's owner, and sometimes also with their coat of arms as with several examples here, a design that seems to have been particularly in vogue during the late 16th and early 17th centuries.

Hunting was long seen as a virile occupation and good preparation in the skills of warfare for a warrior elite. As an activity it was unsurprisingly seen as important to help develop the young; for instance, 15th-century chronicler John Hardyng wrote that it could teach hardiness, courage, strategy and mental quickness. Its restriction to the wealthy was based on the cost of hunting birds, which were expensive, as were their care, feeding and the lengthy and specialized training that was required. In turn, the wealthy might lavish much upon their sport with ornate jesses sometimes made of silk strings, and the leather hoods that calmed resting birds by covering their heads, being decorated with embroidery or heraldic colours. It is unsurprising that all the examples here are therefore made in silver. Indeed, in their enthusiasm, some took the sport to almost indulgent extremes: Nicholas de Litlington, Abbot of Westminster, in 1368 bought a wax image of a falcon to offer at the church altar as an *ex voto* for the health of a sick falcon.

© Norfolk Museums Service
(Norwich Castle Museum
& Art Gallery)

Young Peregrine Falcon with hawking jesses

© Norfolk Museums Service
(Norwich Castle Museum
& Art Gallery)

Iranian Lustreware Hawk

The grandeur of this rare and spectacular sculpture is a testament to the importance of falconry in Medieval Middle Eastern societies. Treatises on the sport of falconry were written in the Middle East at an early date, and their knowledge transmitted to Europe. This Iranian hawk shows clearly how these magnificent birds were, and still are, regarded with admiration, awe and respect. A figure like this one, an artistic and technical masterpiece, would have been a status symbol in itself, presumably commissioned as an indication of its original owner's enthusiasm for falconry.

FAMILY **Accipitridae (Hawks, Eagles, Kites, Harriers and Old World Vultures)**
ORDER **Accipitriformes (Diurnal Birds of Prey)**

Figure of a hawk,
c. 1179–1198
© The Fitzwilliam Museum, Cambridge

Portait of Emperor Jahangir with Hawk

This portrait of the Mughal Emperor Jahangir (1569–1627) shows him holding a hawk wearing a ruby round its neck. The ruby was an especially highly valued gem in Mughal Indian society, believed to symbolize power and strength. Jahangir had a fondness for white falcons and mentions one favourite in his diary. It is possible that this painting represents this particular bird.

Falconry was an ancient pursuit in India and a popular sport among Mughal nobility. Jahangir was unusual in being not only a keen falconer and hunter but also an enthusiastic naturalist with a great interest in birds. His court housed a zoo, and he kept regular notes of his creatures' behaviour. His aviary included what were for the time rare and exotic species, such as a cock Turkey (*Meleagris gallopavo*) and a Dodo (*Raphus cucullatus*).

The Emperor was as fond of the arts as he was of natural sciences, and fine art flourished during his reign. Mansur (*fl.* 1590–1624), who excelled in portraying flora and fauna, became Jahangir's court artist, and was awarded the title *Nadir al-Asr*, 'the wonder of the age'. Mansur's work stands out amongst artists of natural history worldwide, with his combination of delicately detailed observation and rich and sensitive colouring. Jahangir notes in his memoirs that he thought Mansur 'unique' and, whenever he found a bird, animal or plant of particular interest, he would request Mansur to paint it for his collection.

Portrait of Emperor Jahangir with Hawk, c. 1605–1627
© The Trustees of the British Museum

Birds and Landscape

(including Anseriformes, Gruiformes, Charadriiformes and Pelecaniformes)

Birds can be closely associated with our ideas of place and as such may be strongly connected with local identities. This is especially true in East Anglia, which boasts a wealth of unparalleled natural habitats. The region's position jutting into the North Sea means that it is incredibly important for migrating birds – making it a haven for 'Birders', wildlife photographers and nature lovers alike. This section focuses mainly on the birds that are a well-loved feature of these East Anglian landscapes, especially of the Broads and other wetlands.

The coastal wetlands of north Norfolk are extremely significant and varied habitats, and the National Trust nature reserve at Blakeney is an important site for breeding seabirds. Equally, the mudflats of Breydon Water, west of Great Yarmouth, are home to huge numbers of wintering waders and waterfowl that can exceed 100,000 individuals. The *RSPB* manages Breydon Water along with the nearby Berney Marshes reserve.

These reserves protect an area of wet grassland, intertidal mud and saltmarsh, and are managed for all their wildlife, especially breeding and wintering birds.

The Broads are a network of shallow rivers and lakes found mostly in east Norfolk, but they extend south into Suffolk. The Broads are Britain's largest protected wetland environment and are home to a vast array of wildlife, including many rare water birds, insects and plants. Naturalist, broadcaster and former Keeper of Natural History at Norwich Castle Museum, Ted Ellis (1909–1986) once described the Broads as, "… the breathing space for the cure of souls".

Tibetan Cranes

This watercolour is a 19th-century copy of a painting by Mansur. Renowned in his own day, he proved lastingly influential on later Indian art. Relatively few paintings survive which are known to be by his hand, but there are many copies and adaptations of his style. An unfinished original sketch of these cranes survives in the Victoria and Albert Museum's collection, but the painting is lost, and is known only from this copy.

These cranes are probably portraits of a pair in Jahangir's aviary. They seemed to be among his favourites, and he recorded their behaviour regularly. He was especially intrigued by their devotion to one another, naming them *Laila* and *Majnun*, after a famous pair of lovers in a Persian romance. This painting emphasizes the lasting importance of Mansur as an inspirational wildlife artist, and the reverence in which he was held in later centuries, since his work was copied long after his death.

Grus grus (Common Crane)
FAMILY **Gruidae (Cranes)**
ORDER **Gruiformes (Cranes, Crakes and Rails)**

Tibetan cranes, after a 17th-century original
by Mansur. India, c. 1800

Anglo-Saxon Crane Bone Flute

Animal bones were considered important resources in the past as they could be worked and fashioned into a wide range of objects. In this case the long left tarsometatarsus of a Common Crane has been specially selected for adaptation as an end-blown flute. Crane bones often seem to have been chosen for such pipes, probably because of their size and the natural cavity of the bone. This flute was found in excavations in Thetford in the 1950s, and can be dated to the Anglo-Saxon period (AD 449–1066) on the basis of the rubbish pit in which it was found.

The flute has been trimmed to size and had four holes cut through it, three to act as finger-holes, and one at the other end for a sound-hole. The fipple (or block originally made of wax, clay, wood or bone, that would have directed the blown air precisely across the sound hole) is now missing. The use of three finger-holes is of uncertain significance.

It may be that it allowed the flute to be played with one hand, but there may have been a numerical symbolism too: the magical quality of the number three is known to have been influential in early European instrument design.

Similar flutes are well-enough known from Medieval England. However, this example is one of the earliest known of its type, making it important for reconstructing the types of folk instruments used from at least the Late Anglo-Saxon period.

Cranes were common in the Middle Ages, but became extinct in Britain due to shooting and wetland drainage. In 1979 two cranes found their way to Hickling Broad, and now there is a population of some 20 individuals in the northeast of the Norfolk Broads.

Grus grus (Common Crane)
FAMILY **Gruidae (Cranes)**
ORDER **Gruiformes (Cranes, Crakes and Rails)**

© Norfolk Museums Service (Norwich Castle Museum & Art Gallery)

© Norfolk Museums
Service (Norwich Castle
Museum & Art Gallery)

Romano-British Duck Cups

This pair of beautiful drinking cups is Roman in form but their handles are decorated with 'Celtic'-style swimming ducks. The cups exhibit a fusion of the two separate art traditions and are unparalleled. They were deliberately hidden in the ground during the mid-1st century AD, when the local Iceni tribe rose against the Romans, under the leadership of Queen Boudica.

These cups form part of the Crownthorpe Hoard, which comprised seven bronze vessels, six of which had been crushed and buried inside the largest: a strainer bowl. The others are a patera bowl, a deep saucepan (both of which are Roman imports from Italy) and two shallow bowls. The cups are a closely matched pair of Roman style, with oval bodies and small semi-circular handles. The handles have been enhanced by the addition of ducks, which have eyes inlaid with red enamel.

Together these vessels comprise a drinking set of the type commonly used within a Roman household. The vessels would have been used to strain and serve wine or perhaps ale. Together, the group suggests the adoption of Roman ways by their local owner.

FAMILY **Anatidae (Waterfowl)**
ORDER **Anseriformes (Screamers, Magpie Goose, Ducks, Geese and Swans)**

Babylonian Stone Duck

This simply carved stone from Babylon, at 4,000 years old, is the oldest object in this book. It is thought to have been used originally as a weight to measure grain. Despite this practical use it is far from merely utilitarian. The anonymous ancient sculptor has carved the duck with a keenly observant eye, making use of the natural qualities of the stone. They have pared down the design to its bare minimum while perfectly capturing the form and position of the duck's head tucked into its wing feathers. The end result is timelessly attractive and tactile while, to our eyes, also startlingly modernist in its minimalism. The simplicity that so clearly communicates the essential features of the bird may be compared with the work of 20th-century sculptors such as Constantin Brancusi.

Anas clypeata (Northern Shoveler)
FAMILY **Anatidae (Waterfowl)**
ORDER **Anseriformes (Screamers, Magpie Goose, Ducks, Geese and Swans)**

© Private Collection

© Norfolk Museums Service
(Norwich Castle Museum & Art Gallery)

Allen William Seaby, *Two Peewits*, 1905

Two Peewits

The grandfather of contemporary bird artist Robert Gillmor, Allen W. Seaby (1867–1953) was also a well-known ornithological artist, specializing in woodblock printing in the Japanese style. A man of many talents – in addition to being an artist and print-maker of note – Seaby was also an author and Professor of Fine Art at the University of Reading (1920–1933). His books were on a wide variety of subjects, from children's books about native British pony breeds and historical children's fiction to (perhaps not surprisingly, given his standing at the University of Reading) art history and art techniques.

Seaby learned the techniques of Japanese-style woodblock printing whilst he was a student at Reading under Frank Morley Fletcher (1866–1950). It was Fletcher who first introduced Japanese print techniques to the West. Japanese woodblock printing differs from traditional European woodcut printing (which employs mainly oil-based inks) in that a variety of water-based inks are used to create different transparencies of colour. This approach has been used to great atmospheric effect in Seaby's Lapwing, or 'Peewit' picture – creating subtle shades of blues and greens, and even conveying purples of the iridescent feathers of the birds' rump, scapulars and back.

Vanellus vanellus (Northern Lapwing)
FAMILY **Charadriidae (Plovers, Dotterels and Lapwings)**
ORDER **Charadriiformes (Shorebirds)**

Avocet and Chicks

Robert Gillmor (b. 1936), ornithologist, artist and writer, is a founder member and former president of the *Society of Wildlife Artists*. Following in the footsteps of his grandfather (Allen W. Seaby), he also studied at the School of Fine Art at the University of Reading. Seaby's influence on Gillmor's work can be seen in his use of print-making – Gillmor's favoured medium. He is perhaps best known for his linocut prints which focus on birds and other wildlife, and has illustrated the covers of the *New Naturalist* book series since 1985.

During the 1950s and 1960s the *RSPB* innovatively used works by artists such as Robert Gillmor and Charles Tunnicliffe (1901–1979) for propaganda, recruitment and merchandising. This coincided with, and is said to have contributed to, a large proportion of the dramatic growth in the *RSPB*'s membership from 20,000 to 400,000 over a 20-year period.

The Avocet is, as Gillmor says, "a gift to the print-maker", for its striking black and white colouring. A stylized Avocet forms the *RSPB*'s logo, which was originally designed by Gillmor. Avocets effectively became extinct in Britain in 1840, until a lone pair bred at Salthouse, Norfolk, in 1941. A few years later in 1947 the species became more firmly re-established in East Anglia after continental birds started to breed at the *RSPB* reserves at Minsmere and Havergate Island, Suffolk. One of the most successful species conservation projects ever in the UK, numbers are now up to 7,500 during the winter.

Robert Gillmor, *Avocet and Chicks*, 2003, linocut print on paper
© Robert Gillmor

However, Avocets are classed as having 'Amber' conservation status within Britain, meaning that they are still rare, with at least 20% of the world's population occurring here.

Recurvirostra avosetta (Pied Avocet)
FAMILY **Recurvirostridae** (Avocets and Stilts)
ORDER **Charadriiformes** (Shorebirds)

© Norfolk Museums Service
(Norwich Castle Museum & Art Gallery)

John Sell Cotman (attributed to), *The Bittern*, undated, oil on canvas
© Norfolk Museums Service (Norwich Castle Museum & Art Gallery)

The Bittern

This painting was presented to Norwich Castle in 1949 as a work by John Sell Cotman (1782–1842). However, many features of the work are inconsistent with Cotman's style and the attribution has now been called into question.

This Eurasian Bittern appears to have been caught in its dying moments. The colours are muted, with the exception of highlights picking out the bittern's wings. Pools of light in the distance draw attention to a river (possibly the Yare), and there are glimpses of Norfolk Wherries.

In the early 19th century, when this oil painting was probably painted, bitterns were common in the Norfolk Broads. Today they are very closely identified with Norfolk, especially Broadland. They are probably the first bird everyone associates with this area, even giving rise to the name of the local railway line!

Botaurus stellaris (Eurasian Bittern)
FAMILY **Ardeidae (Herons)**
ORDER **Pelecaniformes (Pelicans, Herons, Shoebill Stork and Spoonbills)**

Bittern Photograph

Emma Turner (1866–1940) was a pioneering figure and one of the first women in wildlife photography. To study wetland birds at close range, she spent much of her time living on a houseboat. This Eurasian Bittern was one of the first known to have hatched on the Broads in the 20th century. Egg collectors and wetlands drainage (amongst other reasons) had led to the bittern's near-extinction by the end of the 19th century. Numbers increased throughout the first half of the 20th century but later dropped again, due primarily to water pollution.

It is thought that, by the 1990s, there were more taxidermy specimens in Norwich Castle than live bitterns in the whole of Britain. Since then, wetland habitats have improved. Figures from the *RSPB* show positive results, with 80 breeding pairs in the UK and 600 birds wintering October–March. Today, the sight of a bittern is a rare privilege for most, but it was once such a common part of Broadland life that it was referred to as the 'Butterbump' (due to its high fat content) and was frequently eaten. It now acts as a symbol of the uniqueness of the Broadland landscape.

Botaurus stellaris (Eurasian Bittern)
FAMILY **Ardeidae (Herons)**
ORDER **Pelecaniformes (Pelicans, Herons, Shoebill Stork and Spoonbills)**

How the bittern defends itself; the upward thrust of the young bird, 1911, from Turner, E.L., *Broadland Birds*, 1924, Country Life

Heron in the Shallows of the Thames

Herons are Maggi Hambling's (b. 1945) favourite birds, which she has portrayed many times. She perfectly captures the grace, sense of speed and streamlined ease of movement of this elegant Grey Heron with rich textures and colours and flickering brushwork. Hambling observes herons in her beloved Suffolk water-meadows, but this heron is shown in the shallows of the Thames. Intended by Hambling to be a comment on the effect of polluted habitats on wildlife, the bird has picked up a mouthful of sewage and is searching in vain for fish. Birds are seen by those who love them as intrinsic, even defining, parts of a landscape. When that landscape is disturbed or despoiled, the effects on local birdlife can be disastrous.

Ardea cinerea (Grey Heron)
FAMILY **Ardeidae (Herons)**
ORDER **Pelecaniformes (Pelicans, Herons, Shoebill Stork and Spoonbills)**

Maggi Hambling, *Heron in the shallows of the Thames*, 2013, oil on canvas, 1219 x 914 mm
© The artist

Migrants and Ocean Travellers

(including Charadriiformes, Procellariiformes and Anseriformes)

In addition to their strong connections with the land, birds are also closely linked with the sea, travel and migration. Some birds travel phenomenal distances annually. The Arctic Tern (*Sterna paradisaea*) holds the record for migration: the longest recorded trip is 35,400 kilometres. The appearance and disappearance of birds at different times of the year seemed highly mysterious until the process of migration was understood. In the ancient world, it was thought that birds hibernated, wintered underwater, or even flew to the moon! Today, ever more efficient satellite tracking devices can monitor the extraordinary journeys of birds. Science is also giving us new insights into the sophisticated means by which birds orientate themselves, finding their way unerringly by the same routes every year.

The poet Ruth Padel asks the question, "where is home for a bird?". Birds' migratory habits can redefine our ideas of homeland.

We may think of Common Cuckoos (*Cuculus canorus*) as typically British birds, but a cuckoo which lives in Norfolk in spring will arrive in Africa three months later, and is equally 'at home' there. On the other hand, groups such as gulls and albatrosses are so much a part of the seascape that they may seem to belong more to the oceans than to any country. They feature in stories of sailors and seafaring worldwide.

East Anglia's coastal environments are vital habitats for birdlife. As a consequence, these areas have always attracted bird lovers and conservationists who devote themselves to maintaining this unique and precious environment.

Yellow-nosed albatross, Ryoei

Bruce Pearson (b. 1950) drew some of his earliest artistic inspiration from the Natural History Galleries at Norwich Castle, but he works in the wild whenever possible, to observe his subjects in their natural environment. He makes sketches, like these seen here of the Yellow-nosed Albatross from the South Atlantic, capturing the birds in every light and at every angle.

For Pearson, art and conservation are inextricably linked. His work reflects his passionate concern to highlight the threat to albatrosses and other seabirds from long-line and trawler fishing. Thousands of birds die annually, caught accidentally in hooks and nets. Albatrosses, which lay only one egg per year, cannot breed fast enough to counter this loss. This has resulted in the 'Albatross Taskforce', an international conservation group, taking urgent action to allay the fast-approaching threat of extinction.

Thalassarche chlororhynchos
(Atlantic Yellow-nosed Albatross)
FAMILY **Diomedeidae (Albatrosses)**
ORDER **Procellariiformes (Tubenoses)**

Tristan wanderer on floor of fish processing plant, Richards Bay, South Africa

The poignant image captured by Pearson shows the fate of many species of the now-endangered albatross – to be killed accidentally as 'bycatch', then discarded onto a fish-factory floor. The painting is made all the more sad because this species of albatross (formerly thought of as a subspecies of Wandering Albatross, *Diomedea exulans*) is now widely recognized as a species in its own right. It was considered 'critically endangered' by the *International Union for Conservation of Nature* as soon as it was discovered by science.

Diomedea dabbenena (Tristan Albatross)
FAMILY **Diomedeidae (Albatrosses)**
ORDER **Procellariiformes (Tubenoses)**

Which Way to Go?

This evocative glass sculpture represents a poignant interaction between nature and humans. A haunting depiction of the Suffolk coast, the inner layer represents the Sizewell nuclear power station, overlaid on the outer dome by etched shorebirds and the characteristic reeds of this unique natural habitat. The outline of a wind turbine may also be seen. The translucent layers of glass allow these elements to be viewed together, the natural overlaid with the man-made.

The title of this sculpture, *Which way to go?*, may not only be a reference to the direction in which the birds are flying, but also suggests a choice for mankind – how we choose to treat the natural world and which way we go in our efforts at co-existence with it. If successful, this depends on a balance, which, as the medium of glass implies, is fragile. In this context, the delicately etched silhouettes of birds and reeds may be contrasted ominously with the looming behemoth of the power station, implying a co-existence that, though maintained at present, has potential for disastrous fracture, with dire consequences for the natural environment.

ORDER **Charadriiformes (Shorebirds)**

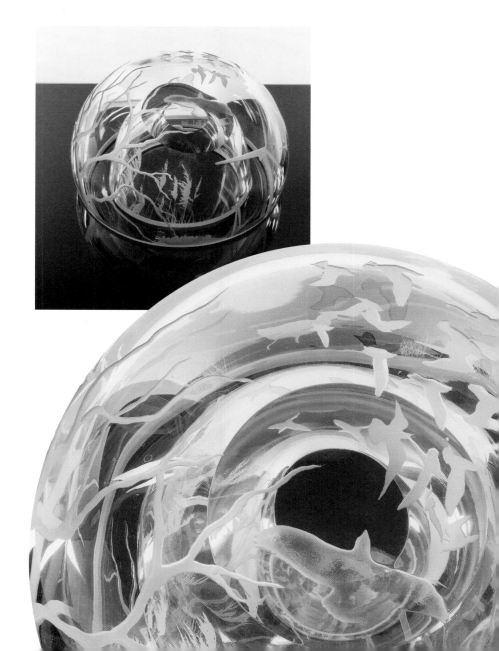

Catherine Hough,
Which way to go?
**2010, blown glass, cut,
sand-blasted and polished**

Arthur Patterson's Cartoons

The naturalist and writer Arthur Patterson (1857–1935) published under the pseudonym 'John Knowlittle'. His unique work documented the wildlife of Breydon Water, east Norfolk, and the disappearing lifestyles of the boatmen, wildfowlers and fishermen who made a living from the estuary. From humble beginnings as the son of a shoemaker in the narrow streets or 'rows' of Great Yarmouth, Patterson made a living in a variety of ways: as a relief postman, warehouseman, salesman, zookeeper and truant officer. But it was as a writer that Arthur Patterson is best remembered. Some of his many book titles include *Notes on Pet Monkeys*, *Seaside Scribblings*, *The Amateur's Zoo*, *Man and Nature on the Broads*, *Notes of an East Coast Naturalist*, *Through Broadland in a Breydon Punt* and *The Cruise of the Walrus*. His 1929 book *Wild Fowlers and Poachers* was dictated to a 17-year-old Ted Ellis at the typewriter. Edward (Ted) Ellis (1909–1986) later became an important and influential natural historian, writer and broadcaster in his own right, and was responsible for starting the longest-running column in a newspaper anywhere in the world – the *Eastern Daily Press* 'In the Countryside' column.

In addition to his books and newspaper articles, Patterson's humorous cartoons became popular features of the local press. He contributed nearly 1,000 cartoons to the *Great Yarmouth Mercury*, *Norwich Evening News* and *Eastern Daily Press* from 1897 until 1914. Patterson was a perennial cartoonist, and in addition to his contributions to the local newspapers, he would also amuse friends and acquaintances with cartoons and sketches on letters and envelopes when he corresponded with them. *Time & Tide Museum of Great Yarmouth Life* has a collection of these sketches, a few of which can be seen here.

Sanderling Photograph and Taxidermy

J. E. (Ted) Knights (*fl*. 1895–1922), of Caister-on-Sea, was apprenticed to Great Yarmouth taxidermist Walter Lowne from 1895. Lowne was a neighbour of naturalist, author and cartoonist Arthur Patterson, who encouraged him to take up taxidermy.

Ted Knights would have had an interesting and varied apprenticeship, as Lowne was privileged enough to preserve rare birds such as several Pallas's Sandgrouse, an Orange-legged Hobby, a Glossy Ibis and an Allen's Gallinule. The latter, a type of rail from sub-Saharan Africa, had flown off course and was captured alive off the coast of Yarmouth! Ted had a mischievous streak – he once played a trick on Lowne by having two owls served for Lowne's supper instead of the moorhens that he had been expecting!

© Norfolk Museums Service (Norwich Castle Museum & Art Gallery)

Chris Knights, *Sanderling Resting*, 2011, photograph
© Chris Knights

Chris Knights (b. 1939) is a well-known wildlife photographer, conservationist and farmer, but he initially gained a reputation as a film-maker after working for Anglia Television's *Survival* series, making films featuring European Hares (*Lepus europaeus*), Grey Partridge (*Perdix perdix*) and Eurasian Stone-curlews (*Burhinus oedicnemus*). Chris now concentrates on still photography, and as well as regularly publishing in books and magazines, he has won *British Birds*' 'Bird Photographer of the Year' three times. A love of natural history runs in the family, as Great Yarmouth taxidermist Ted Knights was Chris Knights' great uncle.

Sanderling visit the UK in winter in order to escape the harsh cold of the High Arctic, where they breed during the summer. Numbers swell to 17,000 birds during the British winter, which means that they have been given 'Green Status' of least concern for conservation by the *RSPB*.

Calidris alba (Sanderling)
FAMILY **Scolopacidae** (Sandpipers)
ORDER **Charadriiformes** (Shorebirds)

Feb. 1964.   BEWICK'S SWANS.   1

10th Feb. 1st in Rushy Pen
♀ Maud
Liaison with Whistler
A rather large pen

11th Feb 1st in Rushy Pen
♂ The Major

11th Feb 1st in Rushy Pen
♀ Ethel (the Speckled Hen)

11th Feb 1st in Rush Pen
Imm ♂ Rudy

11th Feb 1st in Rushy Pen
♂ Aristotle (Onassis)

11th Feb 1st in Rushy Pen
♀ Maria (Callas)

15th Feb 1st in Rushy Pen
♂ Rusty
Aggressive

Original pencil and watercolour drawings by Peter M. Scott
© Dafila Scott

WWT

The Wildfowl & Wetlands Trust

Founded as the 'Severn Wildfowl Trust' in 1946 by Sir Peter Scott, the *Wildfowl & Wetlands Trust* now has over 200,000 members and nine reserves across the UK.

In 1964 Sir Peter Scott and his family realized that each Bewick's Swan bill is unique, and that by recognizing individual birds within a flock you can unlock the secrets of their day-to-day behaviour. At that time, very little was known about these migratory swans' behaviour, no-one was even sure where they migrated to, or how they bred. Combining his skills as an artist and ornithologist, Scott drew the patterns of the swans' beaks in his notebook and so began one of the longest-running research projects of any single species in the world!

Scott's young daughter, Dafila, started to help her father by adding to his drawings, and the position of 'Swan Researcher' has been handed over to several other people since.

As a result of this study, we now know much more about the formerly elusive species. From mid-May every year they arrive in their breeding grounds in the coastal lowlands of Siberia. By the end of September they leave the Arctic and head to western Europe, including East Anglia, around the Severn estuary and Lancashire.

Cygnus columbianus bewickii (Bewick's Swan)
FAMILY **Anatidae** (Waterfowl)
ORDER **Anseriformes** (Screamers, Magpie Goose, Ducks, Geese and Swans)

Dafila Scott, *Bewick's Swans feeding on harvested sugar beet*, 2014, pastel
© Dafila Scott

Bewick's Swans feeding on harvested sugar beet

The Bewick's Swan, named after Thomas Bewick, winters in the UK before leaving in March to breed in Siberia. East Anglia provides important habitats for this migratory swan, and many pass through the *Wildfowl & Wetlands Trust* site at Welney, in the west Norfolk fens.

Artist and zoologist Dr Dafila Scott (b. 1952) has had a lifelong relationship with Bewick's Swans, beginning when she helped her father, Sir Peter Scott, identify and draw swans' bills at WWT Slimbridge Wetland Centre, Gloucestershire.

This atmospheric pastel portrays swans from a 200-strong flock feeding in a field near Welney on a winter afternoon. As a whole, however, the species is declining in western Europe and a number of reasons are being investigated, including collisions with power lines, climate change, lead poisoning and illegal shooting.

Cygnus columbianus bewickii (Bewick's Swan)
FAMILY **Anatidae (Waterfowl)**
ORDER **Anseriformes (Screamers, Magpie Goose, Ducks, Geese and Swans)**

Frank Southgate, *Scoters in Flight*, undated, watercolour on paper
© Norfolk Museums Service (Norwich Castle Museum & Art Gallery)

Scoters in Flight

Frank Southgate (1872–1916) was passionate about shooting and painting the wildfowl of north Norfolk, and was said to go everywhere with both gun and sketchbook. He is most closely associated with the traditional wildfowling 'capital' of Norfolk, Wells-next-the-Sea. The extensive knowledge of both birds and terrain required for wildfowling informed Southgate's art, and his work is full of realistic observation and love of the birds and their habitats. His work and his technique were later greatly admired by Sir Peter Scott.

This watercolour depicts an exuberant flight of Common Scoters, dramatically outlined against a rich blue sky. These seaducks are most often seen in Scotland, Wales and along the Norfolk coast. Unfortunately Common Scoters are not so common today; the species has declined so drastically they are now the subject of an *RSPB* research project. They are vulnerable to oil pollution, but the core reasons behind their plummeting numbers are not yet fully understood.

Melanitta nigra (Common Scoter)
FAMILY **Anatidae (Waterfowl)**
ORDER **Anseriformes (Screamers, Magpie Goose, Ducks, Geese and Swans)**

Introducing the Exotic

(including Psittaciformes, Galliformes, Passeriformes and Gruiformes)

Exotic birds have always been coveted for their brilliant plumage and for their rarity value, for their feathers and as high-status pets. From the 17th-century use of parrots as the exotic centrepiece of a still-life painting, to the detailed Victorian ornithological studies of birds in newly documented parts of the world, birds have dazzled us with their endless variety of forms, feathers and colours.

Portrayals of birds in fine and decorative arts were perennially popular, but one aspect of this fascination with birds has had a serious disadvantage. Real awareness of the possibility of extinction began to dawn on the western world during the 19th century. It had become fashionable to wear not only a feather plume on a hat, but to sport entire capes of feathers, whole hummingbirds pinned to ostrich feather fans, to trim clothing with the feathers of the Osprey (*Pandion haliaetus*), egrets, grebes, Indian Peafowl (*Pavo cristatus*), swans, herons, birds-of-paradise, and many others. The resulting deaths of thousands of birds led to protests in the UK and the USA that culminated in the founding of the *RSPB*.

The use of feathers in fashion continues today, although endangered species are protected and trade in wildlife is controlled. Most feathered fashion accessories are now made from domestic birds' feathers. However, since feathers can now be replicated in man-made materials, continued use of real feathers understandably still causes controversy.

Domesticated birds such as Chickens (*Gallus gallus domesticus*), Turkeys (*Meleagris gallopavo*) and Canaries (*Serinus canaria domestica*) were once as exotic as parrots and hummingbirds. Canaries, today so associated with Norwich and its football club, were brought from the Canary Islands to Europe. Chickens, descended from Red Junglefowl (*Gallus gallus*), are now arguably the most familiar and important birds on the planet. They provide food, both eggs and meat, for millions.

Earthenware Parrot, Staffordshire, 1750s

The fashion for porcelain birds and animals was inaugurated around 1730 by the Meissen factory, the first porcelain manufacturer in Europe. Meissen produced exquisite porcelain sculptures modelled from life for its royal patron, Augustus the Strong, Elector of Saxony. Augustus wanted sculptures of several hundred birds and animals from his private menagerie. This would have represented a spectacular union between nature and art in the fashion of the day.

Due to technical difficulties, many of these models were never made, but other manufacturers soon copied the trend for animal sculptures. Vultures and parrots, painted in great naturalistic detail, were popular Meissen productions, but were so expensive as to be out of reach of all but the wealthiest. This Staffordshire earthenware parrot is clearly a response to the courtly trend from Europe. The parrot, made in a mould rather than hand-modelled and thus a much simpler, cheaper object, nonetheless retains something of the lively character of the original bird. It would have allowed a middle-class consumer to bring the natural world into the home via the newly fashionable medium of porcelain.

FAMILY **Psittacidae (Parrots)**
ORDER **Psittaciformes (Parrots)**

© Norfolk Museums Service
(Norwich Castle Museum & Art Gallery)

Umbrellas

Umbrellas had a somewhat irksome origin within British culture. Commonly used in Europe in the early 17th century, umbrellas didn't make it to the UK until the 18th century. As late as the 1750s umbrella carriers in London were verbally abused and even pelted by coachmen, who saw the use of umbrellas as endangering their livelihoods (private coaches were the only covered way to get around town up until then). However, thanks to the unpredictable and often severe British weather, by the 1790s the use of umbrellas by gentlemen caught on. Early umbrellas were heavy and cumbersome – being made of a stout stick covered by thick waxed or oiled cotton. It was the development of ladies' umbrellas and parasols during the early 1800s that ultimately led to the lightweight design we see today.

These two examples of ladies' umbrellas have bird-shaped handles. The Art Deco swan-headed umbrella is carved from cow horn and dates from the 1930s. The parrot-handled umbrella has been carved from wood, painted and glass eyes inserted, capturing the intelligent, quizzical look of an Orange-winged Amazon Parrot perfectly.

Amazona amazonica
(Orange-winged Amazon Parrot)
FAMILY **Psittacidae (Parrots)**
ORDER **Psittaciformes (Parrots)**

Cygnus olor (Mute Swan)
FAMILY **Anatidae (Waterfowl)**
ORDER **Anseriformes (Screamers, Magpie Goose, Ducks, Geese and Swans)**

Paradise Parakeet

The last living Paradise Parakeet was seen in the wild in Queensland, Australia, in 1927. Also known as the Beautiful Parrot/Parakeet (a parakeet is simply the term for a small parrot), the male of the species was especially splendid – with extraordinary iridescent turquoise, aqua, scarlet, black and brown feathers. A lesson in just how quickly a relatively common bird can become extinct due to human activity; overgrazing, land clearance, hunting by collectors and predation by introduced mammals have all been listed as contributing to the demise of this exceptionally pretty parrot.

The 'Norwich specimen' was collected by professional collector Frederick Strange (born in Aylsham, Norfolk, in 1826), who after a trip to Australia in 1851, brought back an adult male 'Beautiful Parroquet'. Oddly, despite being only nine or ten years old, Frederick's son donated this specimen to the 'Norwich Museum' in 1852 (possibly because Frederick didn't want to be seen giving specimens away to museums when it was his livelihood to sell them). Strange met an untimely death in 1854 whilst on a collecting trip to South Percy Island off the Queensland coast. Aboriginals killed him (and three others) when they wandered into their territory.

Psephotus pulcherrimus (Paradise Parakeet)
FAMILY **Platycercidae (Grass Parakeets)**
ORDER **Psittaciformes (Parrots)**

giving nature a home

The RSPB

The Society for the Protection of Birds (later, *The Royal Society for the Protection of Birds*) has its roots in the history of women's dress, specifically the fashion for plumage in millinery. During the second half of the 19th century, against a backdrop of increasing concern over animal welfare, a number of upper-class women highlighted the particular plight of birds killed in vast numbers to satisfy the demands of fashionable dress. Early legislation, such as the *Sea Birds Preservation Act* of 1869, was designed to combat such trends, but in reality – as Barbara Gates suggests in *Kindred Nature* (1998) – simply shifted attention to the trade in other more exotic birds. "In just one year in the 1880s …" explains Gates, "… over 40,000 West Indian and Brazilian birds and 350,000 East Indian birds were sold on the London market".

The early development of the society was unique in that women dominated its leadership. Indeed, this female leadership shaped its campaign from the outset, with the language and tone of publicity material appealing explicitly to women's sense of vanity and to their role as mothers. Writing in the periodical *The Nineteenth Century* in 1900, the female contributor, Guendolen Ramsden, makes the following impassioned appeal to women's consciences: "it is cruel to wear egret feathers… each of these beautiful birds, whose unfledged young have to die of starvation, supplies one-sixth of an ounce of 'useful' plumage that women may wear. It is said this year that owls are added to the already long list of birds killed only for women's vanity".

A BIRD OF PREY.

Linley Sambourne's cartoons, which appeared in *Punch* magazine in the 1890s, reflect these concerns and provided a much-needed catalyst for the organization. They have subsequently become some of the most enduring images of the campaign. The belief that women would readily respond to this plea, however, proved short-sighted. It took many more years of campaigning before people – including government – took heed, with the *SPB* receiving the Royal Charter in 1904 and the *Plumage (Prohibition) Act* finally coming into force in 1921, restricting the import of birds into the UK.

Feather Hat

The use of feathers for human dress and adornment is ancient and worldwide. As we have seen on the previous page the potentially fatal implications for bird species were first realized in Europe in the 19th century, when a trend for both feathers and whole birds to decorate every type of fashion accessory led to a backlash that culminated in the foundation of the *RSPB*.

Feathers continued to be used during the 20th century and into the present day. This 1960s cloche hat is made of both brightly dyed and natural pheasant feathers. This may have been intended to represent a more acceptable and less damaging alternative to using the feathers of genuinely exotic species.

This style of hat is similar to the cloche of the 1920s and 1930s, close fitting to the head with a dipped brim. These particular feathered styles with overlapping natural and dyed feathers were popular for formal events in the 1960s, and were often worn principally by older women. They were not high fashion, but gave an air of classic elegance to a formal ensemble.

Phasianus colchicus (**Common Pheasant**)
FAMILY **Phasianidae (Pheasants, Partridges, Junglefowl and Peafowl)**
ORDER **Galliformes (Gamebirds)**

Feather Pelerine Cape

Popular in the 19th century, small capes or pelerines would have been worn by women over their outer garments as accessories to carriage or walking dress. This style of pelerine was in fashion during the 1830s when large gigot sleeves created a broad-shouldered silhouette on which to display elaborate capes and collars. The striking alternating horizontal stripes of feathers give an exotic feel to the garment – however, most feathers are either from British native species or common introduced birds such as Eurasian Jay (*Garrulus glandarius*), Common Pheasant (*Phasianus colchicus*) and Helmeted Guineafowl (*Numida meleagris*).

Peacock Ceramic Panel

Peafowl are birds with a wealth of symbolic meaning in cultures worldwide, but in Britain during the late-Victorian period they were most of all icons of Aestheticism, appearing in many forms in fine and applied art.

Birds featured frequently in William De Morgan's ceramic design, and peacocks (male peafowl) were among his favourites. Reflecting their importance in Eastern as well as Western cultures, peacocks were often prominent in the Middle Eastern ceramics that were De Morgan's principal design sources. Peacocks appeared many times in his ceramics, as decoration for both vessels and tiles. His vibrant 'Persian' glaze colours, especially the rich turquoise for which he was so well known, were ideally suited for the artistic interpretation of this bird. In this tile panel De Morgan makes the most of the aesthetic (and Aesthetic) qualities of the peacocks' shapes, enlarging the crests on their heads and entwining their long flowing tails in an exuberant and elegant enjoyment of their form. This panel is a superb example of De Morgan's work and as a paradigm of how the peacock was used in the context of the decorative arts during this period.

Pavo cristatus (Indian Peafowl)
FAMILY **Phasianidae (Pheasants, Partridges, Junglefowl and Peafowl)**
ORDER **Galliformes (Gamebirds)**

William Frend de Morgan,
Tile panel with blue peacocks, *c*. 1888–1898
© The Fitzwilliam Museum, Cambridge.

Fowl

Melchior d'Hondecoeter (1636–1695) was one of
the earliest Western artists to specialize in portrayals
of birds, particularly domestic fowl. His work was
very popular in Britain, and he was notable both
for his lively observation and for his dynamic
compositions. Hondecoeter took the portrayal
of birds beyond the usual 'still life' approach
current at the time. Although his work was
often commissioned for decorative purposes,
he endowed his subjects with great individual
character and depicted them as interacting
dramatically with each other, often with symbolic
meaning. *Fowl* is particularly splendid for its
exuberant cock – his magnificent red plumage and
upright stance as he appears almost to stride out
of the canvas, epitomize the bold personality of the
bird, and contrast with the softer colours and more
passive postures of the seated hens behind him.

Fowl reminds us that cocks and hens, although
now commonplace domestic creatures,
are also exotic species
derived from hybrids
of Red Junglefowl
(*Gallus gallus*) and
Grey Junglefowl
(*Gallus sonneratii*).
Hondecoeter depicted
the most prestigious
and unusual species
of fowl of his day,
even though he
portrayed them in
farmyard settings.

Melchior d'Hondecoeter (1636–1695), *Fowl*, date unknown
© Nottingham City Museums and Galleries NCM 1904-90

Gallus gallus domesticus (Domestic Chicken)
FAMILY **Phasianidae (Pheasants, Partridges,
Junglefowl and Peafowl)**
ORDER **Galliformes (Gamebirds)**

© Norfolk Museums Service (Norwich Castle Museum & Art Gallery)

Canary Medal

Canaries take their name from the Canary Islands, where they were originally found. However, Norwich was once a 'City of Canaries'. Brought by immigrants from the Low Countries in the 16th or 17th century, canaries became popular pets. Canary breeding was an important activity in Norwich until well into the 20th century.

The Mackley family of Norwich was famous for breeding canaries. Jacob Mackley (1850–1923) was regarded as a national authority on the bird. As 'Mackley Brothers' of Philadelphia Lane, he shipped canaries worldwide. In the early 1900s, he sent more than 10,000 birds to the USA alone every year. When he opened his aviaries to the public for three days, 10,000 people came to view the canaries. This medal of 1907/1908 may be a show prize presented by the Mackleys, or it may commemorate these popular open days.

Norwich canaries are known as 'Type Canaries', as they were originally bred for their shape and size, as opposed to 'Colourbred Canaries' or 'Song Canaries'. There are two main forms of the Norwich canary breed – the 'Norwich Plainhead' and the 'Crested Norwich'. The birds depicted on the front of this medal are two crested and a plainhead. The other side shows the Mackley Brothers' moulting room – at the time, a state-of-the-art facility for up to 1,200 birds. Canaries moult every summer and need warmth and a good food supply to produce the best show plumage. Coloured substances are sometimes added to canary food in order to enhance the colour of their feathers – cayenne pepper is traditional!

Serinus canaria domestica (Domestic Canary)
FAMILY **Fringillidae (True Finches)**
ORDER **Passeriformes (Perching Birds)**

Norwich Plainhead Canary

Crested Norwich Canary

INTRODUCING THE EXOTIC

The Realms of the Spirit

(including Passeriformes, Columbiformes, Galliformes, Apodiformes and Cuculiformes)

A bird can both fly and sing. Birds' ability to inhabit the air is an age-old source of mystery and wonder. Although today we fly in aeroplanes, the ancient tale of Icarus, who so spectacularly failed to fly, may indicate the human longing that accompanies the idea of flight. We can all fly in our dreams: birds do so in reality.

In contrast to gorgeously coloured exotic birds, many songbirds are unremarkable 'Little Brown Jobs'. Their wonder is not in their appearance but in their exquisite sound that, as in the case of the Nightingale (*Luscinia megarhynchos*), may be heard while the bird remains unseen. Composers are inspired by birdsong, and poets have used it to symbolize joy, love and sorrow. The harsh cawing of crows and ravens has inspired fear and awe, which translates into particular traditions surrounding these birds. The Tower of London ravens still have their wings clipped so they cannot escape and leave London unprotected!

The qualities of song and flight lead to birds' central place in magic, religion and folklore. They may symbolize the soul, become messengers from heaven or magical beings moving between worlds. Spiritual flight by shamans and mystics is important in many world religions.

Birds have also been heralds of the changing seasons. Sights and sounds of various species are inextricably linked in our minds with certain times of the year, and their occurrence is celebrated in folk customs and festivals. Norfolk naturalist Robert Marsham (1708–1797) from Stratton Strawless, pioneered the science of Phenology. He analysed '27 Indications of Spring' annually, from 1736 until 1797. His family continued the practice until 1956. This Norfolk village therefore has the longest record in the world of the dates of the first Cuckoo (*Cuculus canorus*) call, the sight of the first Swallow (*Hirundo rustica*) and similar signals. In these days of climate change and increasing environmental threat, noting signs like these is more important than ever.

Ravens

This early Anglo-Saxon pendant found in Norfolk is thought to be a representation of the god Woden, with two ravens as the 'horns' of his helmet. Ravens are significant in most of the religions and mythologies of northern Europe. According to the Icelandic Edda poems, the Norse god Odin/Woden, sometimes known as the 'raven god', had two ravens Huginn and Muninn ('Thought' and 'Memory') as his messengers. He sent them out daily to bring him news from around the world, thereby becoming all-seeing and all-knowing. This has been connected to the shamanic religious practices of Northern Tradition religions, since the same principle applied. By identifying with the birds and shape-shifting into bird-form, the practitioner could see with a 'bird's-eye view'.

© Norfolk Museums Service
(Norwich Castle Museum & Art Gallery)

The raven was also sacred to the god Apollo and several bronze figurines showing this bird sitting upon a globe have been found in northeast Norfolk (see above). The remains of iron shanks fixed to the bottom of the globes show that they seem to have formed the tips of sceptres used in religious ceremonies. The localized distribution strongly suggests that this cult, presumably dedicated to a British version of Apollo, was confined to this area. Interestingly, the Roman name for Brancaster – Branodunum – translates as 'Raven Fort'.

Corvus corax (Common Raven)
FAMILY **Corvidae (Crows)**
ORDER **Passeriformes (Perching Birds)**

© Norfolk Museums Service
(Norwich Castle Museum & Art Gallery)

Seal Matrices

In the Medieval period, seal matrices were used to impress a sealing in wax attached to documents. These bore a wide variety of images, and the inscriptions encircling the central device often gave the owner's name or provided a suitable motto.

Birds (both wild and domestic) featuring in the everyday life of the men and women who used these matrices, provided popular subject matter. Sometimes, these referenced the profession of the owner, as with the first seal which carries a depiction of a cock and names its owner as 'Alan the Poulterer'.

Other seals also give clues to the name of their owner, but the bird may be used as a pseudo-heraldic blazon. An example from Coxwold in North Yorkshire names Galfridus (a Medieval version of Geoffrey) of Ulverston in Cumbria. He must have lost this matrix far from home since Coxwold is 120 kilometres from Ulverston as the crow flies, and much further by road.

Another seal from Gloucester shows either a predatory bird attacking another bird, or a male bird attempting to mate with a disobliging female of the same species. The inscription, *Alas le su Pris*, translating as 'alas I am taken', refers to the scene, and can be understood on several levels. The risk of sudden death in an age when disease and violence were ever-present facts of life might be one allusion, but it is also possible that the motto refers to the all-consuming power of love.

© Private Collection

Left to right:
Alan the Poulterer Seal Matrix
Galfridus Seal Matrix
***Alas le su Pris* Seal Matrix**

© Private Collection

© Private Collection

Top to bottom:
Augustine Briggs token;
Thomas Crown token;
Richard Freeman token
© Private Collection

Bird Tokens

During the English Civil War (1642–1651) production of copper coinage ceased and was not resumed until 1672. Thus, from the late 1640s to the early 1670s there was an acute shortage of small change in Britain. This problem was remedied by traders issuing their own unofficial farthing tokens. These display a wide range of designs but some feature birds.

Augustine Briggs was a Norwich grocer who is buried at St Peter Mancroft Church in the city centre. He employed a cockerel on his tokens as he probably operated from an inn in Norwich called 'The Cock'.

Thomas Crane of Great Yarmouth (east Norfolk) used the visual pun of a crane as his token symbol dated 1664, whilst Richard Freeman of Norwich issued pieces with a dove holding an olive branch in its beak. Since doves can symbolize freedom, this may also be a reference to his name.

Gallus gallus domesticus (Domestic Chicken)
FAMILY Phasianidae (Pheasants, Partridges, Junglefowl and Peafowl)
ORDER Galliformes (Gamebirds)

Grus grus (Common Crane)
FAMILY Gruidae (Cranes)
ORDER Gruiformes (Cranes, Crakes and Rails)

FAMILY Columbidae (Pigeons and Doves)
ORDER Columbiformes (Pigeons and Doves)

Flight Takeoff

This extraordinarily original and technically demanding work is part of Geoffrey Mann's 'Long Exposure' series. The artist is intrigued by the idea of capturing in material form the ephemeral qualities of movement and the invisible wave patterns made by creatures in flight. This sculpture depicts a solid trace echo of a bird flying across a room.

The shapes made by a pigeon during take-off, flight and landing were captured using stop-motion cinematography. The images were formed into a continuous shape via computer modelling, and finally cast in glass. The result is a beautiful sculpture which at first seems abstract, but within which the haunting image of the bird may be seen at each end.

Kiln-casting is a technique seldom used by glass artists in the UK, so there was no kiln large enough in the country to fire this highly ambitious work. Mann therefore went to the Czech Republic. The piece took a month to fire in the kiln.

The work is reminiscent of the pioneering pictures produced by Victorian photographers such as Étienne-Jules Marey and Eadweard Muybridge (coincidentally both 1830–1904). Marey's 1890 volume entitled *Le Vol des Oiseaux* (The Flight of Birds) was an astonishing achievement given the technology of the day, as he managed to record several phases of flight on one photographic surface.

Columba livia (Feral Pigeon)
FAMILY **Columbidae (Pigeons and Doves)**
ORDER **Columbiformes (Pigeons and Doves)**

Geoffrey Mann, *Flight Takeoff*, 2008, photographs by Sylvain Deleu
© Norfolk Museums Service (Norwich Castle Museum & Art Gallery)

Flying pelican photographed by Étienne-Jules Marey *c*. 1882

Pelecanus onocrotalus (Great White Pelican)
FAMILY **Pelecanidae (Pelicans)**
ORDER **Pelecaniformes (Pelicans, Herons, Shoebill Stork and Spoonbills)**

Dove

A dove is an almost universally recognized symbol of peace. Made as Picasso's (1881–1973) response to the ending of WWII, his attendance at the Peace Congresses of 1949–1950 and his commitment to Communism, this is a work of both political and personal significance to the artist. Picasso was first taught to paint doves by his father. He also named his new-born daughter 'Paloma', Spanish for Dove, just after he made this work.

Picasso's *Dove* is an acknowledged masterpiece of lithography. The velvety black ink and the simple composition emphasize the bird's dramatic whiteness. The bird shines like a beacon, reflecting optimism and hope for the future. At the same time the softness of its outline and the grey tones of its feathers reflect the fragility both of the dove itself and of the peace it represents.

Picasso's interpretations of the dove, a bird he portrayed many times, are some of the world's best known. They reflect the international importance of this bird's symbolism.

Columba livia domestica (Domestic Dove)
FAMILY **Columbidae (Pigeons and Doves)**
ORDER **Columbiformes (Pigeons and Doves)**

Spring Cuckoo

Norfolk-based Harriet Mead, president of the *Society of Wildlife Artists*, is noted for her unique sculptures of birds and animals in steel, combined with found metal objects such as farmyard tools, horseshoes, keys and scissors. The results are striking, both stark and witty, capturing the essence and strength of the creature. This Common Cuckoo sculpture, incorporating shears, a fork, chain and other found objects, is a highly accurate representation of the species, while the spring upon which it stands is a visual play on the well-known symbolism of the cuckoo as a herald of spring. Mead's art is underpinned equally by her love of wildlife and her passion for conservation. She always intends her work to foreground contemporary issues surrounding each of the species she portrays. Here, despite the cuckoo's 'springing' exuberance, she may also be reminding us of this bird's increasing rarity.

Unfortunately the 'Common' Cuckoo is not as common as it used to be, as it is one of Britain's fastest-declining migrant species. Over the last 25 years there has been a decline of around 50% of breeding cuckoos in the UK. Cuckoo numbers are even worse in England where numbers are down by 63%. Until 2011 no one knew very much about what happened to cuckoos once they left the country to migrate south in early summer (returning the following spring). In a groundbreaking study by the *British Trust for Ornithology* (based in Thetford, Norfolk), lightweight satellite-tracking devices were fitted to cuckoos from Norfolk in order to find out more about their migration routes to and from Africa. The results so far show that the 16,000 kilometre round trips made by 'British' cuckoos are extremely hazardous. Droughts, summer storms and the not insignificant task of crossing the Sahara Desert, all play their part.

Cuculus canorus (Common Cuckoo)
FAMILY **Cuculidae (Cuckoos)**
ORDER **Cuculiformes (Cuckoos, Turacos, Coucals, Roadrunners, Anis and Hoatzin)**

Harriet Mead,
Spring Cuckoo, 2009, metal
© The Artist

Paul Nash, *Mansions of the Dead*, 1932, graphite and watercolour on paper
© Tate, London 2014

Mansions of the Dead

This enigmatic illustration by Paul Nash (1889–1946) forms a unique interpretation of *Urne Buriall.* In this famous work of 1658, Norwich doctor and philosopher Thomas Browne meditated on death, concluding that the only hope of human immortality lay in faith in God rather than in worldly achievements. Nash however interpreted Browne's work in light of his own preoccupations.

The lattice structures and complex interstitial spaces that Nash often featured in his paintings could here be interpreted as the boundaries and cage-like restrictions of life. Nash was much preoccupied with birds and the ability to fly, and believed that after death the soul would take flight like a bird towards heaven. In this work the lattices shift and part, allowing the space to be increasingly inhabited by sky. In the distance, gravity-defying pylon-like structures form a pathway upwards, stretching above the clouds and beyond the range of vision. Bird forms within disc shapes appear to be skimming through the air at high speed, negotiating all obstacles to proceed ever onward.

For Nash, birds symbolized the soul and it is significant that in this work his birds most closely resemble swifts – birds that live almost entirely in the air. Nash's imagery seems serenely optimistic about death, and this picture illustrates perfectly how birds symbolize the human desire for transcendence.

FAMILY **Apodidae (Swifts)**
ORDER **Apodiformes (Swifts, Tree Swifts and Hummingbirds)**

David Tipling,
Murmuration of Starlings, Gretna, Scotland, 2012
© David Tipling

Murmuration of Starlings

Internationally known wildlife photographer David Tipling (b. 1965) has travelled the world in search of many wonderful species, but this extraordinary image was taken in Scotland. Starlings flock in this way at early evening during the autumn, as a means of communication and protection, prior to finding themselves a roosting spot for the night. Murmurations can occur in towns and cities as often as in rural areas, and can occasionally be seen in the centre of Norwich, above Norwich Castle and City Hall. In this photograph the overwhelming spectacle of the murmuration moving in an undulating wave is captured just at the moment when the thousands of starlings seem to be forming into the shape of one single giant bird. Despite the large numbers seen in a murmuration, giving the impression that starlings are numerous, in fact they are in serious decline. The UK's population has fallen by 70% in recent years.

Sturnus vulgaris **(European Starling)**
FAMILY **Sturnidae (Starlings)**
ORDER **Passeriformes (Perching Birds)**

Dave Evans,
Starling, 2014,
linocut
© Dave Evans

Jonathan Clark, Assistant Conservation Officer, cleaning hummingbirds for *The Wonder of Birds* exhibition

Taxidermy Conservation

In order to make sure every object looks its best and is in a fit and stable condition for a new exhibition or publication, many hours of work need to be completed behind the scenes. Specialist conservators (not to be confused with conservationists, who also feature in this book!) use gentle and reversible treatments to stabilize materials. They often use techniques that help to prevent further damage or decay – known as 'preventative conservation'. A code of ethics is followed in order to guide the work being done, as too much intervention results in 'restoration' rather than conservation.

Although well used to working on paintings, frames, ceramics and archaeological material, conservators rarely work on natural history specimens such as taxidermy. Indeed, throughout most regional museums in Britain, it is the natural history curators' job to conserve the specimens in their care. *The Wonder of Birds* was a chance for natural history curators and conservators to swap conservation techniques, and come up with new ideas about the conservation of our natural heritage through museum objects.

One such example is this case of over 140 hummingbirds destined for display in *The Wonder of Birds* exhibition. The glass, plaster and gilded case containing a plethora of hummingbird taxidermy specimens were the perfect mix for traditional object conservation and natural history conservation techniques. Each of the tiny birds had their feathers cleaned using soft brushes, cotton wool, blotting paper and solvents, and wings or heads which had fallen off due to historical pest damage, were reattached. With so many birds to work through, the simple but ingenious system of attaching a brightly coloured cotton thread to treated birds meant that everyone knew exactly at what stage the conservation was!

Many different and perhaps surprising techniques are used in taxidermy conservation, and never let it be said that a curator's work isn't varied and interesting! From using make-up brushes to dust a condor, to cosmetic sponges to clean a cockatoo, ingenuity, trial and occasional error, all played their part!

Grey Crowned Crane undergoing conservation work for *The Wonder of Birds* exhibition

© Norfolk Museums Service
(Norwich Castle Museum
& Art Gallery)

Glossary

Achaemenid Empire – or First Persian Empire, was an empire in western and central Asia, founded in the 6th century BC by Cyrus the Great. At its height in around 500 BC, the empire stretched as far as the Indus Valley in the east to Thrace and Macedon on the northeastern border of Greece in the west, and Egypt in the south.

Aestheticism – or the Aesthetic Movement, is an art movement devoted to the pursuit of the beautiful. Its basic principle is that beauty is where other principles such as morality ultimately derive.

Anzû – a half-man half-bird demigod or monster of Ancient Sumerian legend, the personification of the southern wind and thunderclouds.

Apex predator – predators with few or no predators of their own, existing at the top of their food chain.

Aves – the scientific class containing all birds (living and extinct), including fossil forms such as the Enantiornithes and *Archaeopteryx*. Birds are characterized by having feathers, wings, two legs, and high growth and metabolic rates.

Avian dinosaur – dinosaurs that have feathers, can fly (or their ancestors could) and survived the extinction event at the end of the Mesozoic Era. Synonym of the class Aves.

Bycatch – unwanted fish and other marine creatures trapped by commercial fishing nets/lines whilst fishing for a different intended species.

Cameo – a raised relief image carved or engraved into a gem, semi-precious stone, or shell, where the relief image is a contrasting colour to the background.

Casque – an enlarged horny growth on the beaks of species of birds, such as Hornbills and Cassowaries. From the French word for helmet.

Conservationist – a person who works to protect plants, animals and other natural resources through management and preservation of the natural environment. A person involved in conservation.

Conservator – a professional working on the conservation of cultural heritage, especially museum objects and artwork.

Crownthorpe Hoard – seven vessels buried together at Crownthorpe, southwest of Norwich, discovered in 1982. Some vessels originated in southern Italy, while others exhibit native Celtic-style decoration. Together they comprise a complete Roman-type drinking set, but exhibiting a fusion of Roman and Celtic forms. The assemblage dates from the mid-1st century AD.

Cuir-bouilli – a type of boiled leather often used in Medieval armour. Water, oil, wax or urine were used in the process, allowing the leather to be moulded for a short time after boiling, drying hard but brittle.

DDT – dichlorodiphenyltrichloroethane. An organochloride insecticide first widely used during World War II to help control malaria and typhoid vectors.

Dinosauria – the order of animals also known as dinosaurs, which consists of either *Triceratops*, *Megalosaurus*, and/or *Iguanodon*, Neornithes (modern birds), their most recent common ancestor, and all descendants. Birds are recognized as being the sole surviving lineage of theropod dinosaurs.

Edda – a collection of Old Norse poems and prose that is the most extensive source of Norse mythology. They were written in the Icelandic language in Iceland during the 13th century, but contain material from much earlier Viking Age sources.

Endemic – an organism's ecological state of being indigenous solely to a specific geographical location, such as an island or country.

Extant – the opposite of extinct. A species of biological group still in existence.

Ex voto – short form of *ex voto suscepto*, meaning 'from the vow made'. A votive offering made to a saint or God in a church or chapel where the worshipper wishes to give thanks.

Fipple – the mouthpiece common on many end-blown flutes, such as tin whistles or recorders.

fl. – abbreviation of the Latin word *floruit*, meaning 'he/she flourished'. Used in biographical texts to denote the span of an artist's career.

Fossil Record – the record of the occurrence and evolution of living organisms through geological time as inferred from fossils.

Gigot sleeve – or leg o'mutton sleeve. A type of sleeve extremely wide over the upper arm and narrow along the lower arm. Popular in women's fashion of the 19th century.

Gular pouch – an area of featherless skin forming a pouch stretching from the bottom of a bird's mandibles to its neck.

Heraldry – the system by which coats of arms and other armorial bearings are devised, described and regulated.

Hippogriff – an Ancient Greek and Roman legendary creature with the body of a horse and the head and wings of an eagle.

Iceni – an Iron Age, Brythonic tribe inhabiting an area roughly the same as the modern county of Norfolk.

Integument – the outer protective layer or covering of an animal, such as skin or scales.

Lazarus taxa – the plural of Lazarus taxon.

Lazarus taxon – an organism that disappears from the fossil record, or is recorded as being extinct, only to appear again later (in reference to the Gospel of John, in which Jesus raised Lazarus from the dead).

Low Countries – a coastal region of northwestern Europe, made up of Belgium, The Netherlands, the French Gravelines, Dunkirk and Thionville, and German Eastern Frisia.

Mercer – a merchant or trader who deals in textiles.

Mughal – the Islamic Mughal Empire extended over large parts of the Indian subcontinent from 1526 to 1857. The Mughal Emperors were of central Asian origin, being ultimately descended from Mongol ruler Genghis Khan.

Murmuration – the collective noun for starlings. The name given to the dense clouds of sometimes thousands of starlings in the autumn, as they wheel, swoop and turn together in the sky before roosting.

Nadir al-Asr – 'Unequalled', 'miracle' or 'wonder of the age'. The title bestowed upon Mughal artist Ustad Mansur by the fourth Mughal Emperor Nur-ud-din Mohammad Salim (1569–1627), known as Jahangir.

Needle lace – a type of lace made by creating hundreds of small stitches using a needle and thread.

Neognathae – one of two Superorders of living birds (the other being Palaeognathae). Containing all living birds save for the Ratites and Tinamous.

Neornithes – also known as modern birds; the subclass containing the most recent common ancestor of all living birds (class Aves) and all its descendants. Modern birds are characterized by toothless beaks and high growth and metabolic rates.

Non-avian dinosaur – now extinct dinosaurs that lived during the Mesozoic Era. Dinosaurs excluding the class Aves.

Norfolk Wherry – a type of boat found on the Norfolk Broads, with a single large distinctive, high-peaked sail, and mast set towards the bow of the boat.

Ornithology – the zoological study of birds.

Palaeognathae – one of two Superorders of living birds (the other being Neognathae). Containing the flightless Ratites (Ostriches, Rhea, Cassowary, Emu, Kiwi) and the Tinamous.

Palaeontology – the scientific study of prehistoric life.

Patera – a type of shallow bowl or dish with a distinctive bulbous projection at its centre. Used in certain religious acts in ancient Greece and Rome.

Pelerine – a type of woman's cape popular in the 19th century. From the French word *pèlerine*, meaning a female pilgrim.

Pietre dure – an inlay technique using cut and polished stones to create images.

Ratite – a group of large flightless birds within the order Palaeognathae, consisting of Ostriches, Rhea, Cassowary, Emu, Kiwi, and the extinct Elephant Birds and Moa.

Reformation – a 16th-century movement in western Europe for the reform of abuses in the Roman Church, ending in the establishment of the Reformed and Protestant Churches.

Regalia – the decorations, insignia and ceremonial clothes of any office or order.

Restoration – the art and science of restoring old or damaged objects back to their original or near-original condition.

Rows – the narrow streets that until the 19th century made up much of the Norfolk coastal town of Great Yarmouth. They came about because building was only permitted within the Medieval town walls, and so space was very limited. During WWII many Yarmouth Rows were destroyed or pulled down.

Sauropod – large long-necked non-avian dinosaurs, with thick pillar-like legs, including *Brachiosaurus*, *Diplodocus* and *Apatosaurus*, and the largest land animal ever to have lived – *Argentinosaurus*.

Simurgh – a huge bird-like creature often depicted as having the head of a dog (or sometimes of a human), the paws of a lion and the body of an eagle or peacock. The mythical animal featured mainly in Greater Iranian art and literature, but also appeared in Medieval Armenia, the Byzantine Empire and the Turkic culture of Central Asia.

Slip – clay suspended in water used to decorate the surface of ceramic ware.

Tarsometatarsus – the lower leg bone of birds and some non-avian dinosaurs. Homologous to the tarsus and metatarsus in other animals.

Transitional fossil – a fossil exhibiting characteristics common to both ancestral and derived descendant groups. Because of the fragmentary nature of the fossil record, transitional fossils cannot be assumed to be the direct ancestors of more recent groups (although they are often used as proxies for direct ancestors).

Urne Buriall – *Hydriotaphia*, *Urn Burial*, or a *Discourse of the Sepulchral Urns lately found in Norfolk*, is a work written by Sir Thomas Browne in 1658 as the first part of a two-part work that concludes with *The Garden of Cyrus*.

Vertebrate – any of a large group of animals (around 64,000 species known to science) distinguished by the possession of a backbone/spinal column, including mammals, birds, reptiles, amphibians and fishes.

Vervel – or hawking ring. Used as part of the leather straps attached to a hawk's legs to enable them to be tethered to a stand or hawking gauntlet. Also used as an early form of bird ring, in order to identify ownership of the hawk.

Zoology – the biological study of animals.

18th degree mason – although only three degrees exist within traditional Freemasonry (Entered Apprentice, Fellowcraft and Master Mason), within the 'Ancient and Accepted Rite for England and Wales and its Districts and Chapters Overseas' there are a further 30 degrees or levels of rank.

Further Reading

Aindow, R. 2010. *Dress and Identity in British Literary Culture*, 1870–1914. Ashgate

Birkhead, T. 2011. *The Wisdom of Birds: an illustrated history of ornithology*. Bloomsbury Publishing

Birkhead, T. and van Grouw, K. (illustrator) 2012. *Bird Sense: what it's like to be a bird*. Bloomsbury Publishing

Bottinelli, G. (editor) 2013. *A Vision of England: paintings of the Norwich School*. Norwich Castle Museum & Art Gallery

Cheke, A. and Hume, J. P. 2008. *Lost Land of the Dodo: an ecological history of Mauritius, Réunion & Rodrigues*. Yale University Press

Cocker, M. and Mabey, R. 2005. *Birds Britannica*. Chatto & Windus

Cocker, M. and Tipling, D. 2013. *Birds and People*. Jonathan Cape

Dyke, G. J. and Kaiser, G. (editors) 2011. *Living Dinosaurs: the evolutionary history of modern birds*. Wiley-Blackwell

Elphick, J. 2008. *Birds: the art of ornithology*. Scriptum Editions

Fowler, D. and Eckley, S. (editors) 1996. *The Archive Photographs Series: the Wildfowl & Wetlands Trust*. The Wildfowl & Wetlands Trust

Fuller, E. 2000. *Extinct Birds* (2nd edition). Oxford University Press

Gillmor, R. 2006. *Cutting Away: the linocuts of Robert Gillmor*. Langford Press

Hume, J. P. and Walters, M. 2012. *Extinct Birds*. Poyser

Irmscher, C. (editor) 1999. *John James Audubon: writings and drawings*. The Library of America

Lambourne, M. 2001. *The Art of Bird Illustration: a visual tribute to the lives and achievements of the classic bird illustrators*. Eagle Editions

Magee, J. 2009. *Art of Nature: three centuries of natural history art from around the world*. The Natural History Museum, London

Moore, A. and Thofner, M. (editors) 2010. *The Art of Faith: 3,500 years of art and belief in Norfolk*. Norwich Castle Museum & Art Gallery

Morris, P. A. 2010. *A History of Taxidermy: art, science and bad taste*. MPM Publishing

Olsen, P. 2007. *Glimpses of Paradise: the quest for the Beautiful Parakeet*. National Library of Australia

Page, R. (editor) 2002. *The Feather and the Furrow: the bird photographs of Chris Knights*. Bird's Farm Books

Pearson, B. 2012. *Troubled Waters: trailing the albatross, an artist's journey*. Langford Press

Samstag, T. 1988. *For the Love of Birds: the story of the Royal Society for the Protection of Birds, 1889–1988*. Royal Society for the Protection of Birds

Scott, P. (editor) 1992. *The Art of Peter Scott: images from a lifetime*. Sinclair-Stevenson

Thackray, J. and Press, B. 2004. *The Natural History Museum: nature's treasurehouse*. The Natural History Museum, London

Thatcher, K., Collins, I. and Waterhouse, D. M. 2011. *Wildfowling at Wells: the world of Frank Southgate*. Wells Local History Group

Tooley, B. 1985. *John Knowlittle: the life of the Yarmouth naturalist Arthur Henry Patterson*, A.L.S. Wilson-Poole

Tudge, C. 2008. *Consider the Birds: who they are and what they do*. Allen Lane

Websites

artscouncil.org.uk
audubon.org
birdlife.org
britishmuseum.org
brucepearson.net
bto.org
catherinehough.com
chrisknightswildlife.com
chrispackham.co.uk
dafilascott.co.uk
davidordkerr.com
davidtipling.com
erichoskingtrust.com
fitzmuseum.cam.ac.uk
friendsofthenorwichmuseums.co.uk
harrietmead.co.uk
hawkandowl.org
julianhume.co.uk
maggihambling.com
markcocker.com
mrmann.co.uk
museum.zoo.cam.ac.uk
museums.norfolk.gov.uk
nationalgallery.org.uk
nhm.ac.uk
norfolk.gov.uk
norfolkwildlifetrust.org.uk
rspb.org.uk
swla.co.uk
unfeatheredbird.com
wildlifetrusts.org
wwt.org.uk

Bird species index

Featured artist index

Acknowledgements

From the initial concept to the final exhibition and accompanying publication, *The Wonder of Birds* has been nearly four years in the making. An unbelievable amount of work has been contributed to the project, including research and development, label writing, photography, loans brokering, exhibition design, PR and marketing, publication design, text-panel writing, events and talks development, leaflet design, book writing, educational programmes, object mount making, framing and conservation work. Numerous people have played their part in *The Wonder of Birds*, and thanking all of them individually is unfortunately beyond the scope of this section. I would very much like to thank everyone involved in *The Wonder of Birds*, with the following worthy of special mention.

First I would like to thank the *Friends of Norwich Museums* for the grant that made publishing this book a reality – put simply, without the help and support of the *FNM* committee and members this publication would not exist. I am grateful to our partner organizations for allowing us to reproduce images of their wonderful objects in order to make a lasting legacy of *The Wonder of Birds* project – *The British Museum*, *Eric Hosking Charitable Trust*, *Fitzwilliam Museum*, *Cambridge*, *The National Gallery, London*, *Natural History Museum, London*, *Nottingham City Museums & Art Galleries*, *Tate*, *University Museum of Zoology, Cambridge*, *University of Liverpool Victoria Gallery & Museum*, and the *Victoria and Albert Museum*. I am also grateful to the individual artists and private lenders – Dave Evans, Robert Gillmor, Maggi Hambling, Dr Julian Pender Hume, Clare Jarrett, David Ord Kerr, Chris Knights, Harriet Mead, Bruce Pearson, Christopher Penn, Dr Dafila Scott, Dr Moss Taylor, David Tipling and Katrina van Grouw. Special thanks to Maggi Hambling for allowing us to use the striking image of her heron weathervane and turn it into *The Wonder of Birds* logo.

I am very grateful to Lin Murray and David Gittens from the *Hawk and Owl Trust*, David North of *Norfolk Wildlife Trust*, Matthew Howard, Joanne Hand and Jessica Bygrave from *RSPB* (Eastern England region), Dr Dafila Scott and Mark Simpson from the *Wildfowl & Wetlands Trust*, and Charlotte Crawley and Angela Dunn from the *East Anglia Art Fund*.

I would particularly like to thank Chris Packham for taking time out of his busy schedule to write a poetic and captivating foreword, George Nobbs, Leader of *Norfolk County Council*, for his appropriately 'Norfolky' preface, and Steve Miller, Head of *Norfolk Museums Service*, for his support of the project. Dr Francesca Vanke must also be thanked, as the other major contributing author of this book and lead curator for *The Wonder of Birds* exhibition; her vision and experience in creating compelling exhibitions put us in very safe hands throughout the project. Of course I must also thank the other authors for their contributions: Ruth Battersby-Tooke, Dr Giorgia Bottinelli, Dr John Davies, Dr Rosy Gray, Lisa Little, Dr Adrian Marsden, Dr Tim Pestell and Chris Wood.

I am greatly indebted to former Senior Curator of Natural History at *Norfolk Museums Service*, Dr Tony Irwin, for his mentorship and for his knowledge of birds, as well as to *Norfolk Museums Service* Research Associate Dr Peter Hoare, for giving up his time to act as proof-reader for this book. Other colleagues who deserve thanks include exhibition co-ordinator Fi Hitchcock for working behind the scenes on image credits and copyrights of loans, and especially Paris Agar who always goes above and beyond the call of duty, coming in early, working late and working weekends.

I would also like to thank Malcolm Crampton, Kaarin Wall and the team at *Jigsaw Design & Publishing* for their not insignificant contribution to the design and layout of this book, but also David Kirkham and Neil Jinkerson for providing wonderful photographs.

Bill and Francesca Makins deserve a special mention – their knowledge of birds and ornithological art, coupled with their sheer enthusiasm for the subject, has been an utter inspiration. Dr Moss Taylor and Chris Knights are also both worthy of special thanks, as their expertise and wisdom have proved invaluable several times throughout the most challenging periods of this project.

Finally this acknowledgement section would not be complete without thanking former Keeper of Art at *Norwich Castle Museum & Art Gallery*, Dr Andrew Moore, for the initial idea of *The Wonder of Birds*, and for having the confidence in my abilities to work with me during the all-important initial stages of development.

Dr David M. Waterhouse
May 2014